FRUIT

FROM SALADS TO TARTS

FRUIT

FROM SALADS TO TARTS

Introduction by
Brian Glover

RYLAND
PETERS
& SMALL

LONDON NEW YORK

DESIGNER Pamela Daniels
EDITOR Sharon Cochrane
PRODUCTION Gemma Moules
PICTURE RESEARCH Tracy Ogino
EDITORIAL DIRECTOR Julia Charles
ART DIRECTOR Anne-Marie Bulat
PUBLISHING DIRECTOR Alison Starling

First published in the United Kingdom in 2006
by Ryland Peters & Small
20–21 Jockey's Fields, London WC1R 4BW
www.rylandpeters.com

10 9 8 7 6 5 4 3 2 1

ISBN-13: 978 1 84597 103 8
ISBN-10: 1 84597 103 5

NOTES
• All spoon measurements are level unless otherwise specified.
• All eggs are medium unless otherwise specified. Uncooked or partly
cooked eggs should not be served to the very young, the very old, those
with compromised immune systems or to pregnant women.
• To sterilize jam jars, wash them in hot, soapy water and rinse in boiling
water. Place in a large saucepan and cover with hot water. With the lid on,
bring the water to the boil and continue boiling for 15 minutes. Turn off
the heat and leave the jars in the hot water until just before they are to
be filled. Invert the jars onto a clean cloth to dry. Sterilize the lids for
5 minutes, by boiling, or according to the manufacturer's instructions.
The jars should be filled and sealed while they are still hot.

A catalogue record for this book is available from the British Library.

Printed in China.

CONTENTS

FABULOUS FRUIT

Fresh fruit, with its fantastic texture and sweet flavour, is one of the healthiest and most diverse and delicious of nature's foods.

INFINITE VARIETY

The huge choice of fruits available to us is quite astonishing. We have fruits from the temperate climates of the world – anciently cultivated fruits such as apples, pears, figs and quinces. There are tropical and hot climate fruits from Africa, Asia and South America such as mangoes, bananas and pineapples; and somewhere in between come the huge selection of citrus fruits and warm-climate quick growers such as melons and kiwi fruits.

Some fruits are wonderfully sweet, others fragrant, still others refreshingly tart. It is this diversity that makes fruit such a valuable asset in any cook's kitchen. Sharp and sour fruits such as lemons, limes, rhubarb and pomegranates enliven our food, lifting and transforming dull flavours, while sweet fruits are a natural source of sugar in puddings, pies and cakes as well as adding a sweet/sour note to countless savoury dishes and salads.

SWEET PERFECTION

Many fruits are at their best eaten in their raw and natural state. An impeccably ripe peach, a buttery soft mango, a swollen fig just on the point of bursting – these are fruits for enjoying when they are at the peak of their perfection, letting the juices drip down one's chin. They need nothing doing to them to improve their natural flavour and texture.

At the other end of the spectrum are fruits that only reveal their delights when cooked: amber-pink quinces; pears stained purple after long, slow baking in red wine; sour cherries; shocking pink rhubarb and tart damson plums. All these need a little heat, as well as a sprinkling of sugar or honey to make them good to eat, but your patience will be rewarded with a depth of flavour that often outshines that of raw fruit on its own.

In between these two extremes there is a huge number of fruits that can be enjoyed both raw and cooked. Sometimes the application of just a little warmth, a sprinkling of sugar or a squeeze of tart citrus will transform a dull fruit into something quite mouthwatering. Papaya cries out for lime juice; lacklustre strawberries are transformed with a squeeze of orange juice or passion fruit; apricots have a remarkable affinity with vanilla and green gooseberries with the muscat flavour of elderflowers. Fruits such as guavas, starfruit and physalis reveal unexpected flavours when gently cooked with a little sugar.

SERVING FRUIT

One of the very best ways to round off a meal is to offer a large platter of the best fresh fruits you can find. It might be a mixture such as wedges of nectar-sweet pineapple and buttery mango or a branch of rose-flushed lychees and a cluster of muscat-scented grapes. Or it might simply be a huge china bowl of irresistible dark red cherries or of purple-black figs laid on a bed of their own leaves. If you live near a farmers' market, a tray of heritage variety aromatic apples and pears or a bowl of juicy plums and greengages can do nothing but delight.

But read on for more inspiration. Getting the best out of fruit is what this book is all about, giving you a large selection of recipes and ideas to make use of what is probably the most varied and enjoyable group of fresh, natural foods we have at our disposal in the kitchen.

FRUIT BASICS

With so many varieties available from all over the globe, fruit is one of the most exciting and diverse culinary ingredients we have. Whether your passion is for lemons or lychees, melons or mangosteens, this tour of the immense and varied world of fruit will help you to get the maximum enjoyment out of all the different types. There is also information on choosing, storing, preparing and cooking fruit, as well as highlighting the health benefits of this fantastically versatile food.

CITRUS FRUITS

Oranges, lemons and limes are an essential element of any cook's alchemical storecupboard. Their delicious blend of sweet fragrance and tart sourness makes it hard to imagine cooking in the modern kitchen without them.

Until the 17th century, LEMONS were little used in Western cooking. Like all citrus fruits, they originated in China and came to Europe only in the early medieval period when they were used in medicine and as preservatives. The availability of cheaper sugar in the 17th century meant that lemon's acid-drop sharpness could be tamed and lemon became one of the world's most popular flavourings. LIMES have a richer, warmer taste than lemons and work particularly well with spicy flavours such as chilli, ginger and galangal. Kaffir limes (*Citrus hystrix*) have headily fragrant leaves and zest that are much used in Thai food.

Sour ORANGES were brought to Europe from China in the 11th century. At first, bitter oranges were used in medicine and perfumery, but with the arrival of sweet varieties from China in the 17th century, the orange was well on its way to becoming the world's favourite fruit. Its popularity partly due to its ripening during the northern hemisphere's winter, providing an invigorating burst of healthiness in an otherwise dreary diet at that time of the year. Navel and Valencia varieties are particularly good and ruby-stained blood oranges from Italy and California are sweet and juicy.

Citrus fruits are remarkably promiscuous and interbreed freely. Growers now concentrate on breeding sweet, juicy fruit that's easy to peel, seedless and smaller than the average orange. The

TANGERINE is really a generic name for the different kinds that have small segments and fragrant loose peel. SATSUMAS are Japanese in origin; MINEOLAS are hybrids of tangerines and grapefruit so are a little larger and slightly less sweet. (UGLI FRUIT come from the same cross but are larger and misshapen.) CLEMENTINES are a cross between a tangerine and an orange and generally the smallest fruits have the most exceptional flavour. They all make great ices and deep-flavoured preserves and are an essential part of most northern Christmas celebrations.

The GRAPEFRUIT is one of the larger citrus fruits – a West Indian hybrid between the pomelo and sweet orange. White grapefruit is noticeably tart, while red and pink grapefruit are sweeter. The latter can be used in salads with no extra sugar and go well with avocado, smoked fish or shellfish. The POMELO is a larger citrus fruit with dryish, less juicy flesh. CITRON (*Citrus medica*) has thick peel that's often candied for use in cakes.

The KUMQUAT is a different species from other citrus, but will interbreed with them. The tiny fruits can be eaten skin and all. They have a pure, sharp orange flavour and are delicious briefly cooked in a sugar syrup with vanilla or orange-flower water. They are also good in salsas, chutneys and marmalades. A cross between kumquats and limes, LIMEQUATS are tart and need more sugar in cooking.

BERRIES, CURRANTS AND SOFT FRUITS

Sweet, red berries are the essence of summer – imagine a bowl of juicy strawberries and sun-warmed raspberries for breakfast on a fine summer's morning.

The STRAWBERRY we know and love is a truly international creation. It was bred in France and England in the 18th and 19th centuries from wild varieties from the east coast of North America and the Pacific coast of South America. Now, the modern strawberry has conquered the world. Growers have always sought to breed larger fruit but the small, wild Alpine strawberry and *fraise de bois* have a special intensity – when you can find them.

RASPBERRIES flourish in cooler, damper climates than strawberries and in many varieties. Those that fruit in autumn and amber-coloured, yellow raspberries are particularly sweet and intense. Of all the berries, raspberries make possibly the best jams and sweet preserves.

Strawberries grow on stumpy little plants, while raspberries like to aim high on long, annually-produced canes. In between the two is the wild bramble, a stout colonizer of rough ground that bears intense purple, lip-staining fruits. Cultivated BLACKBERRIES are larger than their wild relation, the bramble, and are sweet enough to eat raw. Both make superb pie fruits, either by themselves or with apples. There's a host of berries related to raspberries and brambles: from North American DEWBERRIES, LOGANBERRIES and BOYSENBERRIES to Japanese WINEBERRIES, Scottish TAYBERRIES and the golden-hued CLOUDBERRIES from Arctic Europe and Canada. All make a good pie.

GOOSEBERRIES are hardy, northern fruits that grow on inhospitable, thorny bushes. They are either eaten when acid-drop green and sour or when they have ripened into sweet berries barely containing their juiciness in a thin red-stained skin. In France, gooseberries are known as *groseilles à*

maquereau – a name which suggests how these tart fruits can be served as sauces to fish like mackerel. They also go well with salmon or, indeed, goose.

BERRIES are made for pies and tarts. Whether a tumble of strawberries on a French open tart or homely pies bursting with brambles, soft fruits and home baking go hand in hand. Perhaps the most popular is the BLUEBERRY and its wild relation, the mountain BILBERRY. Bilberries are wonderfully intense, but cultivated blueberries are much plumper and juicier. Blueberries can lack flavour raw but brief cooking and a little sugar effects a Cinderella-like transformation.

Most CURRANTS also benefit from a little heat and sugar to release their musky flavour. Opalescent WHITECURRANTS and garnet-coloured REDCURRANTS are wonderful thrown into a hot, vanilla-scented syrup and left to cool. BLACKCURRANTS are more intense. Packed with vitamin C, they need lots of sugar but produce delicious cordials and pies. Blackcurrants also make some of the best ices and sorbets, capturing the essence of summer in one icy-cold mouthful.

Sealing-wax red CRANBERRIES ripen in the late autumn – just escaping the first frosts of winter. Cranberries grow on low, ground-hugging bushes and are traditionally 'floated' off the plant to form red rafts of colour over the flooded fields of North America. Cranberries and turkey go together like strawberries and cream whether at American Thanksgiving or at Anglo-Saxon Christmases around the world. But, cranberries aren't just for Christmas – they make excellent pies, muffins (page 44) and puddings, especially when flavoured with orange, ginger or port.

RHUBARB

Rhubarb is an anomaly: we eat it as a fruit, but it's really a vegetable – the edible leaf stalk of an otherwise poisonous plant. A native of Siberia, it flourishes in cold climates. In the kitchen, rhubarb needs sugar, though you can use it to make barely-sweetened sauces and relishes for fatty fish and rich meats – Persian cooks add it to a lamb or duck stew called *khoresh*. Also known as 'pie-plant' in the States, rhubarb is essentially used for sweet cooking. It mixes well with strawberries or with ginger, orange or lime in homely pies, crisps and crumbles. But it can also do smart; try rhubarb in fruit compotes with papaya and lime or with pineapple. Best of all, try rhubarb fool made with homemade custard.

ORCHARD AND VINE FRUITS

These are the most anciently cultivated fruits of the temperate world. No other fruits are a product of such human effort and endeavour in breeding and cultivation, with some varieties being centuries old.

A good, ripe FIG is all about texture: its thin skin should barely contain the sweet, jelly-like flesh, allowing the thousand tiny seeds to explode onto the tongue. It is one of the oldest cultivated fruits beloved of the Egyptians, Turks, Greeks and Romans. Thin-skinned, purple-black figs are perhaps the best for eating raw (pages 38 and 51); poach green-skinned figs in a sugar syrup or bake them in fortified wine such as Madeira until they split open. Figs are best eaten sun-warmed straight from the tree, but in the shops choose soft, yielding fruits – a few beads of sugary juice around the stem are a good indication of ripeness.

The DATE palm is another long-cultivated crop – it has been grown for at least 5,000 years in the Middle East and North Africa. Until fairly recently, dried dates were all one could find outside the Middle East but now fresh dates are more widely available. They have a crisp texture and light, sweet flavour, which makes them good for use in salads. The best dates are the medjool variety grown in California and North Africa. They have a toffee-like, brown sugar flavour and an intense, sticky texture and make a delicious after-dinner treat with coffee. Dates are good in cakes and tarts with walnuts or pecans.

APPLES have been grown since classical times and wild crab apples gathered since prehistory. Grafting – the technique by which good varieties are grown on vigorous, wild rootstocks – was known to the ancient Greeks and is still used today. There are thousands of varieties of apple, some dating from the 17th century. Apples ripen over several months and some can be stored through the winter, which historically made them a valuable source of vitamins in the colder months. Today, perfect, crisp apples are available all year round but it is worth searching out heritage varieties from farmers' markets; they vary immensely in flavour, from tan-coloured russets to aromatic pippins. In Europe, particularly Britain, sour apples – such as the famous Bramley Seedling – are valued in cooking.

The Romans were particularly partial to PEARS and took them with them across their empire. Prior to the Romans, the Chinese had been growing pears for thousands of years. But it was the French who, in the 17th and 18th centuries, produced such wonderfully evocative varieties as Doyenne d'Eté and Beurre Hardy. Pears are great mixers – they sweeten tart fruits such as blackcurrants or cranberries and also go well with blackberries and plums. Pears make a great accompaniment for cheese, especially blue or salty cheeses such as pecorino or Parmesan. The best way to deal with hard, unripe pears is to stew them with wine, sugar and spices in a low oven. Asian or Nashi pears are much crisper than European pears and are particularly good in salads.

The QUINCE is another ancient fruit, which resembles a swollen-hipped, knobbly pear covered in a soft, grey down. Quinces are said to have been the golden apples of Greek mythology associated with Aphrodite, the goddess of love. Aphrodite might have swooned at the fragrance – a single, ripe quince will scent a whole room – but she would have been disappointed had she tried eating one raw. They need long, gentle cooking to make them edible; the best fruit will then turn a wonderful amber-pink colour. Quince is used to make *membrillo* – the grainy-textured paste from Spain – that is delicious served with sheep's and goat's milk cheeses, particularly with its traditional partner, Spain's own sheep's milk cheese, Manchego.

There are thousands of varieties of PLUM, from sour wild ones such as sloes and bullaces through the tiny French mirabelles to purple-black damsons and on to the intensely sweet and perfumed greengages. Plums originated around the eastern Mediterranean – damsons get their name from the Syrian capital Damascus – but they reached their height in the 19th century in England when the best-known variety Victoria, named after the then Queen, was bred. Opalescent greengages are widely thought to be the most aromatic of plums. Most varieties, especially damsons, make great preserves and also make a lovely tart baked on a base of rich almond frangipane.

There is something about a sweet, red ripe CHERRY that says, 'Here is summer in one irresistible mouthful'. If you can resist cherries raw (which is hard), they are also wonderful cooked. Poach them in red wine syrup with spices, or pickle them in vinegar and sugar with star anise and cloves. Bake them in French almondy tarts or a crumbly-crusted all-American pie. Sour morello cherries make great jams, while dried cherries have an irresistible fruity-almond flavour.

The perfect PEACH is perhaps the most delicious of all the stone fruits and yet the most elusive as an exquisitely sweet, juicy peach is one of the most delicate, hard-to-transport fruits imaginable. White peaches have an ethereal, rose-blushed attraction and often the best flavour. The warm, downy skin is, for many peach-lovers, part of their appeal, but for those who cannot abide it, the smooth-skinned NECTARINE is heaven sent. Otherwise the two are virtually identical. I love peaches in tarts or pies with redcurrants or blueberries, or halve and stone them, stuff with crumbled amaretti biscuits and bake them as they do in Italy.

APRICOTS have a more intense, muskier flavour than peaches and are less juicy. Most store-bought apricots benefit from cooking. Bake them in the oven with a vanilla pod or some lemon zest and sugar or poach them in a sweet dessert wine. Apricots make lovely fools and ice creams. Like all stone fruits, apricots have a real affinity with almonds (they belong to the same vast *Prunus* family). The best dried apricots are the elusive Hunza variety of central Asia – look out for them in wholefood stores.

Because of wine-making, GRAPES are perhaps the most important of all fruit crops. They are also one of the oldest. Signs of grape cultivation and wine-making in Egypt go back over 4,000 years. In terms of table grapes, the best flavour is often found in those almost translucent, bloomy muscat grapes touched with amber. The tiny red grapes of Greece capture some of the same intensity and sweetness. Grapes are for eating raw – they are delicious in salads and with cheeses – or very briefly cooked so they retain their texture.

MELONS

Nature has never come up with a better way of packaging water and sugar than in a melon. Melons originated in Africa where wild watermelons grow in the Kalahari Desert. They were used by bushmen as a valuable and easily transportable source of water. Columbus took melon seeds to the Americas and they first grew in Haiti. Medieval Europe was enthusiastic about melons, though some held them in deep suspicion. Catherine de Medici was accused of eating so many that they gave her stomach ache and melons were thought too cooling for easy digestion. The habit of serving melon with port or with warm spices such as pepper, chilli or ginger is the modern legacy of this medieval doubtfulness. It is precisely melon's coolness that makes them the most refreshing of all fruits. Orange-fleshed melons such as cantaloupe and Charentais are particularly aromatic and soft. Crisper are the creamy-green fleshed honeydew melons. Chartreuse-green fleshed varieties such as the Ogen and Galia are also well-flavoured and netted or muskmelons have a heady, almost alcoholic muscat perfume. Melons are good in salads with salty ingredients such as feta cheese (page 59) or air-dried ham and they make great smoothies and deliciously aromatic sorbets and ice creams. Melons are rarely cooked; the texture collapses and most of the flavour is lost.

EXOTIC AND TROPICAL FRUITS

Mango and pineapple are among the finest of all fruits but there is an enormous choice of other fruits from tropical and warm climates to beguile you with their exotic scents and flavours.

A ripe MANGO has a soft, melting buttery texture that cannot be matched by any other fruit and to eat one is a gloriously messy business. There are many different kinds: from small, yellow-skinned mangoes shaped like commas to large green, red-flushed ones. They smell delicious when ripe and the fruit should feel heavy and plump. They make the best ices and are delicious in salads and salsas, especially with Thai flavours such as chilli, fish sauce and lime (page 64).

The world divides into those who like their BANANAS firm and underripe and those who would not consider eating them until they are soft and almost squashy. For fruit salads, salsas and fritters (page 125), choose firm bananas; for ice creams and loaf cakes (page 47), the fruit needs to be fully ripe, even touched with brown in places. Red bananas have a fine flavour when fully ripe. Bananas go well with the flavours of rum, cardamom, lime, muscovado sugar, maple syrup, coffee and walnut.

Cut open a PAPAYA to reveal the scented, salmon-pink flesh set off by the grey-black seeds. Its sweet and floral flavour is greatly enhanced by lime juice. Papayas are good in salads with seafood (page 62), with hot, sweet-sour dressings based on lime juice, but they work well with smoked fish or air-dried ham. Green, sharp unripe papayas are worth searching out to make authentic Thai salads. A ripe GUAVA will scent a room; raw, they also need lime juice, but gentle cooking brings out their exotic flavour.

'Discovered' by Columbus in the Caribbean, the PINEAPPLE was a sensation when it first reached Europe. Wealthy landowners grew them in heated glasshouses and decorated their country houses with pineapple sculptures. When ripe, a leaf from the top-knot should pull away easily and the fruit will smell intoxicatingly delicious. A little lime juice or a sprinkling of kirsch can work wonders for a disappointing pineapple.

Native of South America, the PASSION FRUIT is one of the very few tropical fruits that is better used in cooking than eaten raw. The orange pulp inside the purple shell is intensely scented – sweet but with a mouthwatering tartness. It is also full of hard, crunchy seeds – so heat the pulp very gently, then sieve it to remove the seeds. The larger, orange-skinned GRANADILLA is similar but with a less intense flavour. Passion fruits make wonderful ice cream and are perfect with strawberries. Don't reject wrinkled fruit – they often have the best flavour.

LYCHEES are one of the most sensuous fruits, with rough, pink-flushed skins, silky flesh and a beguiling scent and flavour evocative of jasmine tea and rosewater. MANGOSTEEN, LONGANS and RAMBUTANS (which look like a sea urchin) are similar, but the plump lychee is my favourite. They look beautiful served on the stem after dinner for guests to peel and nibble (you may find these in Chinese markets).

PHYSALIS is a pretty fruit with a flavour reminiscent of a ripe dessert gooseberry – hence its alternative name, Cape gooseberry. Serve as a nibble after dinner, or dip them into caramel or a rum-scented fondant icing.

The KIWI vine is a native of China (it was sometimes called the Chinese gooseberry), but it is in New Zealand that the crop really took off, hence the name. Unripe kiwis can be a little bland, but a good one has a sweet flavour reminiscent of strawberries with which, incidentally, they mix very well. Kiwis contain an enzyme that tenderizes meat and fish – try them in marinades for steak, chicken or squid.

STARFRUITS are valued for their prettiness – they are invariably sliced in cross-section to make star-shaped slices to add to fruit salads or to garnish puddings. They have a crisp, green, slightly tart flavour that works well in Asian-style salads. Gentle poaching in sugar syrup brings out the best flavour.

POMEGRANATES are beautiful, ancient fruits. The garnet-hued seeds add a sweet-tart flavour and unique texture to salads and fruit compotes – try them strewn over a dish of baked figs with spices and orange-flower water. Sweet-sour syrup pomegranate molasses is made from the concentrated juice and pomegranate juice flavours grenadine too.

CHOOSING, BUYING AND STORING

The best advice when choosing and marketing for fresh fruit is to follow the seasons and trust your nose more than your eye.

Seasonal fruit, which often means locally-grown fruit, will have had more chance to ripen on the plant so will taste better. Of course, the global market place means that a specific fruit will always be in season somewhere, but the need for transportation often means it is picked before it is fully ripened and this can affect the flavour.

Besides, there is a certain undefinable pleasure in eating fruit at the peak of its seasonal best. Strawberries belong to long, lazy summer days no matter how tempting they are in mid-winter; while clementines and tangerines seem an integral part of winter holiday celebrations.

Farmers' markets are often a good place to shop for locally produced seasonal fruit. Certainly, if you are thinking of making preserves or freezing fruit, buying in season from a fruit farm or a farmers' market makes sense both in terms of flavour and cost.

SELECTING FRUIT

For many fruits, aroma is a good guide to both ripeness and flavour.

• A good **melon**, such as a Charentais, Galia or Ogen should have a strong, almost alcoholic fragrance.

• **Peaches, quinces, strawberries, apricots, plums, raspberries, mangoes, guavas, pineapples** and **bananas** all have heady scents that tell you when they are ripe and ready to eat.

If you get a chance to handle fruit before you buy, go gently so as not to damage it. Fruit should be firm, not squashy or bruised.
- A ripe **melon** or **pineapple** will 'give' a little if gently pressed at one end (though this doesn't work with a hard-skinned honeydew or watermelon).
- **Citrus fruits** that feel heavy will be full of juice. Lemons and clementines bought on the stalk not only look pretty but stay juicier for longer.

In most cases avoid fruits with wrinkled or damaged skins. The exceptions are **passion fruit** – a few wrinkles mean a more intense flavour – and muscat **grapes** and **loquats**, where a few brown spots indicate the sweetest flavour. Colour can be a good indication of ripeness and flavour. The best **apricots** are invariably blushed with red, while **peaches** should have no signs of green. **Pomegranates** are at their sweetest when they turn a burnished red; a ripe, sweet **papaya** turns yellow. Don't always reject green **citrus fruits**, it may be simply that they have not been treated with chemical ripening agents.

Some fruits are at their best when almost overripe. Purple **figs**, golden **persimmons**, downy **peaches**, translucent **greengages** and muscat **grapes** are all best enjoyed at this reckless, just-about-to-go over the edge state of ripeness.

STORAGE

Many of us store fruit in the refrigerator but the cold, dry atmosphere does the flavour few favours.
- Some fruits – noticeably **bananas** – really suffer when stored at cold temperatures. For these and **apples**, **pears** and all **citrus fruits** the fruit bowl at cool room temperature is the best place.
- Even if we have to store delicate fruit in the refrigerator to prevent its spoiling, leave it at room temperature for a few hours or on a sunny windowsill for a few minutes for the best flavour.
- Some unripe fruits will ripen in a warm room or on a sunny windowsill. Try this with **pears**, **bananas**, **apricots**, dessert **gooseberries**, **figs**, **mangoes** and **pineapples**.
- Don't forget the old trick of putting unripe fruits in a paper bag with a banana or apple to help speed up ripening.

PREPARING

The good news is that many fruits are nature's best example of ready-packaged and prepared foods. You need do little more to the perfect apple, pear or peach than give it a gentle rinse. Even fruits that require a little more preparation need only a few basic skills.

WASHING

Fruit that you eat whole and unpeeled will need washing. But treat it gently. Washing summer berries and currants under the full force of the tap can bruise the fruit and dilute flavour. Leave strawberries unhulled until after washing and wash raspberries, blackberries and currants gently by putting them in a colander or sieve, then submerging them in a large bowl of water (don't overcrowd the colander or you will crush the fruit). Let them drain thoroughly, then dry on kitchen paper or clean tea towels.

Citrus fruits are routinely waxed to prolong their shelf life. If you are using the zest from citrus fruits, choose organic or unwaxed fruits. Wash organic fruit in warm water. Scrub regular waxed and non-organic citrus fruits in warm, soapy water before rinsing well and drying.

STONING AND DESEEDING

The stones, pits and seeds of fruits are all removed more easily when the fruit is fully ripe: some out-of-season peaches cling onto their stones whatever you try to do.

• If you are planning to stone a lot of **cherries**, buy a cherry-stoner from a good kitchenware shop – it will save you a lot of time.

• **Mangoes** are notoriously difficult to detach from their stones. Try this: with the mango on its side and using a sharp knife, cut off a thick 'cushion' of flesh from each side of the stone, then cut around the stone to remove as much of the remaining flesh as you can. Alternatively, cut wedges out of the mango, working around the stone.

• **Peaches**, **plums** and **apricots** should be cut in half following the natural crease in the skin. Holding one half, gently twist the other half. A ripe fruit should fall apart and the stone can be pulled out. With small plums, such as mirabelles and damsons, removing stones after cooking is usually simpler.

• Cut **pomegranates** in half, loosen the seeds with a spoon, then invert the fruit over a bowl and tap it sharply with the spoon, the seeds should dislodge themselves and fall into the bowl.

• Ripe **peaches** and **nectarines** can be skinned by immersing the fruit in boiling water for 1–2 minutes. Drain, and the skin should slip off easily.

SLICING

• **Bananas**, **pears**, **apples** and **quinces** brown quickly on slicing. To prevent this, toss them in a little lemon or lime juice as you slice them.

• Slice off the top and bottom of **pineapples**, cut into 6–8 wedges and cut out the core. Cut each wedge off the skin with a small sharp knife and slice the flesh into chunks.

• Cut a slice off the top and bottom of **oranges**. Hold the orange upright on a board and cut off all the peel and white pith in strips working from the top to the bottom. Either slice or, for pith-free segments, cut each segment out from its membrane, folding the membrane back like the leaves of a book as you work. Do this over a bowl to catch the juices.

• Top and tail **gooseberries** using sharp kitchen scissors. If you buy **currants** on the stalk, just pull the stalk through the tines of a fork and the currants will fall off.

COOKING WITH FRUIT

Few fruits demand long or complicated cooking – and most require none at all. A few simple techniques are all you need to get the most out of fruit in your kitchen.

POACHING

This is the method of cooking fruit in a barely simmering liquid, usually with sugar. The heat should be low, so the liquid just bubbles, to make it easier to control the degree of doneness and prevent the fruit from breaking up. Use enamelled or stainless steel pans to poach fruit – acid fruit juices can react with aluminium to discolour fruit and give it a metallic taste.

A good basic syrup for poaching fruit can be made from dissolving 120–220 g sugar in 500 ml water. The sourer the fruit, the more sugar you will need. Wine, cider, spirits and other fruit juices can also be used as the poaching liquid. Flavour the syrup with spices – such as star anise, vanilla pods, cinnamon sticks, cardamom or root ginger – or strips of citrus zest.

Cook the fruit as briefly as possible, until tender but not collapsing, then remove the cooked fruit with a slotted spoon. Boil the syrup fiercely to reduce and intensify it before letting it cool and spooning it over the cooked fruit.

• The skins of **peaches** and **nectarines** will slip off easily once the fruit is cooked.
• Cook **cranberries** in liquid – orange juice is good – without extra sugar. Add sugar only when they pop, otherwise the skin of the fruit will toughen.
• When poaching **quinces**, add the core and pared skin to the liquid to help the syrup turn a glorious sticking-plaster pink.
• Add sliced forced **rhubarb** to a barely simmering syrup. Cook for 1–2 minutes, then cover the pan and remove from the heat. The rhubarb should cook perfectly in the cooling syrup. This works with red- and whitecurrants too.

BAKING AND ROASTING

Long, slow baking is the best way to deal with hard fruits such as unripe **pears** and aromatic **quinces**. Put the peeled, cored fruit (though small pears are nice left whole) in a deep baking dish, cover with hot liquid and add sugar and flavourings. Cover and bake in a low oven until the fruit is meltingly tender – this can take several hours. Reduce the syrup by fast boiling at the end. Serve chilled.

Roasting is much quicker and done at a higher temperature. It works best with fully ripe but still firm fruits such as **figs**, **pears**, **peaches**, **nectarines** and **plums**. Halve and stone the fruit as necessary or leave plums whole. Cut a shallow cross in the top of figs. Pack into a baking dish and sprinkle with sugar or honey, a few spoonfuls of wine or fruit juice and maybe a few knobs of butter. Bake, uncovered, basting with the juices from time to time until the fruit is tender but not collapsed.

A gentler type of baking is good with **apricots**, **rhubarb**, **apples** and **pears**. Put the prepared fruit in a baking dish, with sugar and few spoonfuls of liquid, and whatever flavourings you like. Cover tightly with foil and cook in a medium oven.

HEALTH BENEFITS

Fruit is nature's healthy convenience food, containing water, energy, vitamins, minerals and trace elements all in one tempting package.

GETTING THE MOST FROM FRUIT

Nutritional experts tell us we should be eating more fruit – at least five portions of fresh fruit and vegetables a day. The healthiest way to eat fruit is the simplest – raw and whole. In fruits such as **pears**, **apples**, **plums**, **cherries** and **peaches**, most of the vitamins are either in or just beneath the skin. So by peeling fruits you are throwing away valuable dietary fibre and the most nutritional part.

While fruit juices are invigorating and healthy, remember that the juice of an orange contains only about a quarter of the vitamin C present in the whole fruit and you lose out on fibre too. Blended fruit drinks are much better in this respect – preserving more vitamins and fibre.

All cooking affects the nutritional value of fruit, but a few guidelines can help you get the best out of the fruit you cook.
• If you are slicing or chopping fruit to add raw to a dish, avoid doing this too far in advance to help preserve texture, colour and vitamin C content.
• Tossing cut fruit in lemon juice stops the oxidizing process which affects the colour as well as vitamin content.

• Heating fruit inevitably destroys some of its nutritional content but you can minimize this by cooking fruit for as short a time as possible, by cooking it in the minimum amount of liquid and by cooking it whole wherever possible.

• Many of us try to keep added sugar to a minimum, but it does play an important role in cooking fruit. Not only does it make cooked fruit taste good, it also helps to prevent fruit from overcooking and becoming mushy. Cooking it in natural fruit juices can reduce the amount of sugar needed.

FRUIT FOR HEALTH

Besides fruit's general health benefits, certain fruits have been found to be particularly good for us in a number of specific ways.

• Fruits particularly high in vitamin C, which helps to ward off colds and infections, are **oranges, guavas, kiwi fruit** and **blackcurrants**. Blackcurrants can contain well over 100 mg of vitamin C per 100 g of fruit – most other fruits contain around 10–20 mg per 100 g.

• **Cranberries** contain phytochemicals, which have been shown to inhibit bacterial growth in the urinary system, helping to ward off infections such as cystitis.

• **Blueberries** are a particularly rich source of antioxidants which, research has shown, may help delay deterioration in memory and general coordination.

• Research has shown that the antioxidants in **bilberries** can strengthen the blood supply to the retina, so helping to prevent eye strain.

• **Figs**, especially when dried, are a good source of iron, which helps protect against anaemia.

• **Cherries** contain flavonoid compounds that help to reduce uric acid levels in the body and so may ease the symptoms of inflammatory diseases of the joints such as arthritis and gout.

ANTI-AGEING PROPERTIES

Fruit is generally a good source of antioxidants, especially when they contain anthocyanin pigments. These are the pigments that give fruits like **blood oranges** their colour. They are present in noticeably high levels in **bilberries, blackberries, blackcurrants, blueberries, cherries, cranberries,** red and purple **grapes, strawberries** and **redcurrants**. These anthocyanins work to inhibit and limit the effect of free radicals in the body. It is widely accepted that oxygen-derived free radicals are the underlying cause of cell ageing. Some anthocyanins show anticarcinogenic properties. Most anthocyanins are present in the skin or peel of fruits, which is why red wine – that derives its colour from the skin of red or purple grapes – is considered better for general health than white.

BRUNCH

Fruit makes a deliciously refreshing start to the day. Simply sprinkle berries or other soft fruits over a bowl of cereal to make it more appealing, or fruit can be used to form the basis of an altogether more tempting brunch dish. Whether it's Blackberry Buttermilk Pancakes with Apple Butter or Raspberry Waffles with Peach and Pistachio Honey, fruit is always a welcome morning treat. Fresh Figs with Ricotta and Honeycomb can be prepared in an instant, while for a more comforting brunch try one of the delicious baking ideas such as Warm Blueberry and Almond Muffins or Banana Pecan Loaf – both perfect with a cup of coffee.

Apples and blackberries are great together, and here a buttery apple sauce tops blackberry-dotted pancakes. Use blueberries or raspberries as an alternative.

BLACKBERRY BUTTERMILK PANCAKES with apple butter

APPLE BUTTER

500 g cooking apples, such as Bramleys

3 tablespoons soft brown sugar

a pinch of ground cinnamon

1 teaspoon freshly squeezed lemon juice

25 g butter

PANCAKES

125 g self-raising flour

1 teaspoon bicarbonate of soda

25 g fine cornmeal

40 g caster sugar

1 egg, beaten

350 ml buttermilk, at room temperature

15 g butter, melted

125 g small blackberries, plus extra to serve

oil, for greasing

single cream, to serve

serves 6

To make the apple butter, peel, core and dice the apples. Put in a saucepan with the sugar, cinnamon, lemon juice and 1 tablespoon water. Bring to the boil, cover and simmer over low heat for 15–20 minutes until softened. Mash with a fork, add the butter and heat through, uncovered, until thickened. Remove the pan from the heat, set aside and let cool.

To make the pancakes, sift the flour and bicarbonate of soda into a bowl and stir in the cornmeal and sugar. Put the egg, buttermilk and melted butter in a second bowl and beat until mixed. Stir the mixture into the dry ingredients to form a smooth, thick batter. Fold in the blackberries.

Heat a heavy-based, non-stick frying pan until hot, brush lightly with oil and pour in a little of the batter to form a small pancake. Cook for 2 minutes until bubbles appear on the surface. Turn the pancake over and cook for 1 minute more until cooked through. Transfer to a plate and keep the cooked pancakes warm in a low oven while you cook the remaining batter in batches.

Serve the pancakes warm, topped with a spoonful of apple butter, extra blackberries and a little cream.

These pancakes are perfect when you have a house full of people for breakfast – and they are ideal for a summer morning. Most of the preparation is done the night before, so breakfast is a breeze. The mango and ginger purée takes seconds to prepare.

MANGO AND GINGER PURÉE

2 ripe mangoes, peeled and chopped

3 cm piece of fresh ginger, peeled and grated

freshly squeezed juice of 1 lime

2 tablespoons icing sugar

PANCAKES

300 g plain flour

2 tablespoons caster sugar or vanilla sugar

1 teaspoon easy-blend dried yeast

1 teaspoon salt

375 ml milk

85 g unsalted butter, melted and cooled, plus extra for greasing

2 eggs, separated

TO SERVE

assorted tropical fruit, such as mango, starfruit (carambola), kiwi fruit, passion fruit and papaya

2 tablespoons sesame seeds, pan-toasted in a dry frying pan

a flat griddle pan or frying pan

serves 4–6: makes 10–12

OVERNIGHT PANCAKES
with mango and ginger purée
and tropical fruit

To make the mango and ginger purée, put the mangoes in a blender. Squeeze the grated ginger to extract the juice. Add the juice to the mangoes and discard the gratings. Blend well, then stir in the lime juice, sugar and a little water, if the purée is too thick. Set aside. The purée can be stored, covered, in the refrigerator for up to 2 days.

The night before you want to serve the pancakes, sift the flour, sugar, yeast and salt into a large bowl. Add the milk and melted butter and mix gently to make a thick batter. Cover the bowl and leave at room temperature overnight.

Next morning, put the egg whites in a spotlessly clean, grease-free bowl and whisk with a wire whisk or electric beaters until stiff peaks form. Stir the egg yolks into the pancake batter, then gently fold in the egg whites with a large metal spoon.

Heat a flat griddle or frying pan over medium heat and lightly grease it. When hot, reduce the heat and pour 2–3 tablespoons of batter into the pan to make 1 small pancake. Pour in more batter to make 3–4 small pancakes and cook over low heat for 1 minute until small bubbles begin to appear on the surface and the underside is golden brown. Turn the pancakes over and cook for 2 minutes more until cooked through. Transfer to a plate and keep the cooked pancakes warm in a low oven while you cook the remaining batter in batches.

Serve the pancakes warm, topped with tropical fruit, a spoonful of mango and ginger purée and a sprinkling of pan-toasted sesame seeds.

Not all yeast batters need to be left for hours – you can cheat and still get some great results. The secret is to make sure everything is warm before you start, right down to the flour and the bowl – use the defrost setting on the microwave to raise the mixture in half the time.

SPICY NUT WAFFLES
with ginger pears

285 g plain flour

1 teaspoon easy-blend dried yeast

½ teaspoon salt

2 tablespoons caster sugar

2 teaspoons ground cinnamon

200 g walnuts, finely chopped

310 ml warm milk

1 teaspoon pure vanilla essence

100 g unsalted butter, melted and cooled

2 eggs, separated

GINGER PEARS

½ bottle sweet wine (375 ml), such as orange muscat

120 g sugar

6 cm piece of fresh ginger, peeled and thinly sliced

3 mini pears or 1 large pear per person, peeled

TO SERVE

150 g crystallized or glacé ginger, thinly sliced

natural yoghurt or whipped cream (optional)

a waffle iron, lightly greased

serves 4–6: makes 6–8

Put the flour in a large microwavable bowl and heat on HIGH for 10 seconds – this will speed the rising process. Add the yeast, salt, sugar, cinnamon and walnuts to the warm flour.

Put the warm milk, vanilla, cooled melted butter and egg yolks in a separate bowl and mix well. Add the flour mixture to the milk mixture and stir gently until smooth. Cover with clingfilm and leave in a warm place for 45 minutes until doubled in size.

Meanwhile, to make the ginger pears, put the wine in a saucepan large enough to fit the pears in a single layer. Add 300 ml water, the sugar and ginger and bring slowly to the boil over medium heat. Add the pears, reduce the heat and simmer for 25 minutes, gently turning the pears from time to time to make sure they cook evenly. Using a slotted spoon, carefully remove the pears to a plate. Boil the ginger liquid for 10 minutes to reduce it to a thin syrup. Strain the syrup to remove the ginger, then return it to the pan along with the pears. Set aside to steep until the waffles are ready.

Put the egg whites in a spotlessly clean, grease-free bowl and whisk with a wire whisk or electric beaters until stiff peaks form. Gently fold them into the risen waffle batter using a large metal spoon.

Preheat the waffle iron, then spoon 4–8 tablespoons of the batter (depending on the size of the waffle iron) into the compartments. Cook until golden, 4–5 minutes. Transfer to a plate and keep the waffles warm in a low oven while you cook the remainder. To serve, pour some ginger syrup over each waffle and top with 1 large or 3 small pears, some crystallized or glacé ginger and a spoonful of yoghurt or whipped cream, if using.

These delicate waffles are jam-packed with fruit. As the batter cooks, the raspberries soften and the juice seeps into the fabric of the waffle giving a beautiful red mottled effect.

RASPBERRY WAFFLES
with peach and pistachio honey

PEACH AND PISTACHIO HONEY

2 firm peaches, skinned and stoned

350 ml clear orange blossom honey

1 tablespoon peach schnapps (optional)

50 g shelled unsalted pistachio nuts

WAFFLES

285 g plain flour

2 teaspoons baking powder

½ teaspoon salt

3 tablespoons caster sugar

3 eggs, separated

225 ml milk

55 g unsalted butter, melted and cooled

2 teaspoons pure vanilla essence

150 g raspberries

crème fraîche, to serve (optional)

a waffle iron, lightly greased

serves 4: makes 8

To make the peach and pistachio honey, cut the peach flesh into 3 mm cubes. Put the honey and schnapps, if using, in a saucepan and heat until almost boiling. Remove the pan from the heat, add the chopped peaches and pistachios and let cool slightly.

To make the waffles, sift the flour, baking powder, salt and sugar into a large bowl. Put the egg yolks, milk, cooled melted butter and vanilla essence in a separate bowl and beat well. Add the dry ingredients to the egg mixture and stir until just mixed. Add the raspberries to the batter, crushing some with the back of a spoon to give a marbled effect.

Put the egg whites in a spotlessly clean, grease-free bowl and whisk with a wire whisk or electric beaters until stiff peaks form. Gently fold them into the waffle batter using a large metal spoon.

Preheat the waffle iron, then spoon 4–8 tablespoons of the batter (depending on the size of the waffle iron) into the compartments. Cook until golden, 4–5 minutes. Transfer to a plate and keep the waffles warm in a low oven while you cook the remainder.

Serve the waffles warm, topped with a spoonful of the peach and pistachio honey and some crème fraîche, if using.

There isn't much to beat figs straight from the tree, bursting with sweetness and a sublime flavour. Try to buy figs as ripe as possible for this dish. If they are unavailable, use other fruits such as peaches, apricots or cherries.

500 g fresh ripe figs, about 8

500 g ricotta cheese, sliced

a piece of honeycomb or
4–8 tablespoons honey

serves 4

FRESH FIGS
with ricotta and honeycomb

Arrange the figs and sliced ricotta on a large serving plate. Put the honeycomb or honey in a separate bowl for everyone to help themselves. Serve immediately.

Grinding whole coffee beans with lump sugar is typically
Italian and adds a delicious crunch to this dish. This is a
mouthwatering way to serve peaches, to be enjoyed on
a warm summer morning.

6 large peaches or nectarines

2 tablespoons clear honey

1 tablespoon coffee beans

1 tablespoon lump sugar

300 g chilled ricotta cheese

a baking dish, lined with baking parchment

serves 6

HONEY-ROASTED PEACHES
with ricotta and coffee bean sugar

Cut the peaches or nectarines in half and remove the stones. Put
the peaches or nectarines in the prepared baking dish cut side up.
Drizzle with the honey and roast in a preheated oven at 220°C
(425°F) Gas 7 for 15–20 minutes until the fruit is tender and
caramelized. Remove from the oven and let cool slightly.

Put the coffee beans and sugar in a coffee grinder and work very
briefly until the beans and sugar are coarsely ground.

To serve, spoon the peaches or nectarines onto plates, top with
a scoop of ricotta and a sprinkle of the sugary coffee beans.

This is a simple fruit compote that is best served slightly warm. You can use nectarines instead of peaches if you prefer, plus whatever berries you fancy.

2 unwaxed oranges
3 ripe peaches, stoned and sliced
8–12 apricots, stoned and halved
175 g blueberries
25 g caster sugar
1 cinnamon stick
Greek yoghurt, to serve

serves 4

WARM COMPOTE
with peaches, apricots and blueberries

Peel the zest from 1 of the oranges, removing only the zest and not the bitter white pith. Cut the zest into thin strips and put in a shallow saucepan. Squeeze the juice from both oranges and add to the pan.

Add the peaches, apricots, blueberries, sugar and cinnamon stick to the pan and heat gently until the sugar dissolves. Cover and simmer gently for 4–5 minutes until the fruits are softened.

Serve the compote warm with Greek yoghurt.

Muffins are quick and easy to prepare and make a lovely brunch snack, especially when served warm with coffee. Blueberries make a delicious muffin, but you could replace them with raspberries if you prefer.

WARM BLUEBERRY AND ALMOND MUFFINS

200 g plain flour

1½ teaspoons baking powder

1 teaspoon ground mixed spice

50 g ground almonds

175 g sugar

1 egg

300 ml buttermilk

50 g butter, melted

250 g blueberries

15 g almonds, chopped

a 12-hole muffin tin, lined with 10 paper muffin cases

makes 10

Sift the flour, baking powder and mixed spice into a bowl and stir in the ground almonds and sugar. Put the egg, buttermilk and melted butter in a second bowl and beat well. Stir into the dry ingredients to make a smooth batter.

Fold in the blueberries, then spoon the mixture into the muffin cases filling them three-quarters full. Scatter with the chopped almonds and bake in a preheated oven at 200°C (400°F) Gas 6 for 18–20 minutes until risen and golden. Remove from the oven, let cool slightly on a wire rack and serve warm.

CRANBERRY, ORANGE AND PECAN MUFFINS

150 g plain flour

150 g wholemeal flour

1 tablespoon baking powder

85 g golden caster sugar

50 g pecans, coarsely chopped

grated zest of ½ unwaxed orange

1 large egg

280 ml milk

2 teaspoons freshly squeezed orange juice

4 tablespoons melted butter or vegetable oil

150 g fresh or frozen cranberries (use straight from the freezer)

a deep 12-hole muffin tin, well greased

makes 12

Sift the flours and baking powder into a large bowl, then stir in the sugar, pecans and grated orange zest. Put the egg, milk, orange juice and melted butter or vegetable oil in a separate bowl and beat lightly. Add to the dry ingredients, stirring quickly with a wooden spoon until just mixed. Add the cranberries and stir briefly, using as few strokes as possible. Do not beat or overmix; the batter should look slightly streaky.

Spoon the batter into the prepared muffin tin, filling each hole about two-thirds full. Bake in a preheated oven at 220°C (425°F) Gas 7 for about 20 minutes until golden and firm to the touch. Remove from the oven, let cool in the tin for 1 minute, then turn out onto a wire rack. Eat warm, immediately or within 24 hours. When thoroughly cooled, the muffins can be wrapped and frozen for up to 1 month.

Light and crumbly in texture, crammed with delicious fruit and nuts, this loaf cake is irresistible, especially when served with a steaming cup of coffee for a sweet brunch treat. Use very ripe bananas for maximum flavour.

BANANA PECAN LOAF

125 g unsalted butter, at room temperature

170 g golden caster sugar

2 large eggs, beaten

½ teaspoon pure vanilla essence

400 g very ripe bananas

100 g pecans, coarsely sliced

250 g self-raising flour, sifted

a loaf tin, 1 kg, greased and base-lined

makes 1 large loaf cake

Put the butter and sugar in a large bowl and beat with an electric mixer or wooden spoon until light and creamy. Gradually beat in the eggs and vanilla essence to make a fluffy mixture. Mash the bananas with a fork – they should be fairly coarse rather than a purée. Carefully fold in the mashed bananas, pecans and flour.

Transfer the mixture to the prepared loaf tin and smooth the surface with a palette knife. Bake in a preheated oven at 180°C (350°F) Gas 4 for about 1 hour until golden and firm to the touch and a skewer inserted into the centre comes out clean.

Let cool in the tin for 5 minutes, then turn out onto a wire rack to cool completely. Serve warm or at room temperature, thickly sliced and spread with butter. The loaf is best eaten within 3 days. When thoroughly cooled, it can be wrapped and frozen for up to 1 month.

STARTERS, SOUPS AND SALADS

Fruit can be used in all sorts of chilled soups, to make fresh and delicious salads and little dishes to serve as starters. These recipes take you on a tour of world cuisines. Ripe figs and Parma ham are a heaven-sent combination from Italy, while the Sicilian Orange, Endive and Black Olive Salad makes a refreshing starter or lunch dish. From Thailand there is a Papaya Salad with Squid and Mango Beef Salad. Or try the Mexican-inspired Grilled Chilli Herb Polenta with Papaya Mojo.

The combination of sweet, salty Parma ham and a yielding soft fruit like ripe figs or melon is one of life's little miracles. This is an all-time Italian classic, and none the worse for that. Serve this with a little trickle of aged balsamic vinegar over the figs, if you can find one. It will be thick, sweet and syrupy, and heaven to use in tiny amounts – and it will taste amazing. This is quick to assemble, providing you have excellent, thinly sliced ham and perfect, garnet-centred figs.

4 large or 8 small fresh ripe figs (preferably purple ones)

1 tablespoon good balsamic vinegar

1 tablespoon extra virgin olive oil, plus extra to serve

12 thin slices of Parma ham or prosciutto crudo

150 g fresh Parmesan cheese, broken into craggy lumps

crushed black pepper

serves 4

PARMA HAM WITH FIGS
and balsamic vinegar dressing

Stand the figs upright. Using a small, sharp knife, make 2 cuts across each fig not quite quartering it, but keeping it intact. Ease the figs open and brush with the balsamic vinegar and olive oil.

Arrange 3 slices of Parma ham on each plate with the figs and Parmesan on top. Sprinkle with extra virgin olive oil and plenty of crushed black pepper and serve.

Ripe figs filled with goats' cheese and wrapped in prosciutto make a great first course. Prepare the salad in advance, but add the dressing at the last minute, otherwise it will become soggy.

8 large fresh ripe figs

80 g goats' cheese

8 slices of prosciutto

RADICCHIO SALAD

1 head of radicchio, trimmed

a handful of walnut pieces, pan-toasted

4 tablespoons walnut oil

2 tablespoons extra virgin olive oil

1 tablespoon vincotto or reduced balsamic vinegar*

sea salt and freshly ground black pepper

4 wooden skewers soaked in cold water for 30 minutes

serves 4

FIG, GOATS' CHEESE AND PROSCIUTTO SKEWERS
with radicchio salad

Stand the figs upright. Using a small, sharp knife, make 2 cuts across each fig not quite quartering it, but keeping it intact. Cut the cheese into 8 equal pieces. Put 1 piece of cheese in the middle of each fig, then close them. Wrap each fig with a slice of the ham, then thread 2 wrapped figs onto each skewer.

Preheat the barbecue. Cook the skewers over medium hot coals for 4–5 minutes, turning halfway through, until the ham is charred and the figs are sizzling. Alternatively, cook the skewers on a preheated stove-top grill pan for 4–5 minutes, turning halfway through.

To make the salad, tear the radicchio leaves into pieces and put in a bowl with the walnut pieces. Put the walnut and olive oil, vincotto or balsamic vinegar and salt and pepper to taste in a separate bowl and whisk well. Pour over the radicchio and toss well to coat. Serve with the fig skewers.

*NOTE Vincotto, produced all over Italy, is made by cooking grape must for a long time until it has a honey-like consistency. If you can't find it, use reduced balsamic vinegar. To make this, put 300 ml balsamic vinegar in a saucepan and bring to the boil. Boil gently until it has reduced by about two-thirds and has reached the consistency of thick syrup. Let cool, then store in a clean jar or bottle.

Sweet watermelon tastes amazing blended
with the spicy prickle of dried chilli flakes.
Use the ripest melon you can find.

WATERMELON SOUP
with chilli flakes

1 ripe watermelon, chilled, cut into wedges
1 tablespoon chilli flakes, plus extra to serve
ice cubes, to serve (optional)

serves 4

Cut the seedy part out of each wedge of
melon and transfer to a sieve set over a
bowl. Press the flesh through the sieve
(don't worry too much about getting it
all) and transfer the contents of the bowl
to a blender.

Cut the seedless parts of the watermelon
into large chunks and put them in the
blender, along with any juice.

Blend, in batches if necessary, until smooth.
Add the chilli, blend briefly, then pour into
chilled soup bowls. Add ice cubes, if using,
top with extra chilli flakes and serve.

Use very scented melons, such as green Galia or orange Charentais. Don't chill the melons, or you will deaden their flavour.

ROCKMELON SOUP
with japanese pink pickled ginger

2 ripe cantaloupe- or honeydew-style melons

500 ml crushed ice

1 tablespoon ground ginger

1 tablespoon freshly cracked black pepper

2 tablespoons chopped Japanese pink pickled ginger

sprigs of mint or borage flowers (optional)

ice cubes, to serve

serves 4

Halve and deseed the melons. Using a spoon, scoop out the flesh into a blender or food processor. Add the crushed ice and ground ginger and process, in bursts, to a purée. Add enough iced water to make a pourable consistency.

Pour into chilled soup bowls and add the pepper, pink pickled ginger, mint sprigs or borage flowers, if using, and ice cubes. Serve immediately.

a small bunch of coriander

4 sprigs of oregano

a handful of fresh chives

250 g quick-cook polenta

50 g unsalted butter, cut into pieces

50 g Asiago vecchio or Parmesan cheese, freshly grated

2 long red chillies, deseeded and finely chopped

olive oil spray

sea salt and freshly ground black pepper

PAPAYA MOJO

75 g shallots, thinly sliced

grated zest and freshly squeezed juice of 1 unwaxed lime

5 tablespoons olive oil

1 large papaya, peeled and cut into cubes

a small bunch of coriander

a handful of fresh chives, chopped

EPAZOTE BEANS

100 g dried black beans, rinsed and drained

2 sprigs of epazote or a pinch of dried

a baking sheet or dish, 23 x 32 cm, oiled

a ridged stove-top grill pan

serves 6

Epazote is a Mexican herb, available dried and sometimes fresh in Latino markets. It is famous as a partner for beans, because it counteracts their gaseous tendencies.

GRILLED CHILLI HERB POLENTA with papaya mojo

To prepare the beans, put them in a bowl, cover with cold water and let soak overnight. Drain and rinse, then transfer to a saucepan. Cover with cold water and bring to the boil for 5 minutes. Lower the heat, add the epazote and simmer until the beans are just cooked, about 1 hour. Drain well.

Remove the leaves from the coriander and oregano stalks and chop them coarsely with the chives. In a large saucepan, bring 2 pints water to the boil and add a pinch of salt. Add the polenta all at once, whisking constantly. As the polenta thickens, stir in the butter and cheese. Mix well, then fold in the herbs, chillies, and salt and pepper to taste.

Pour into the prepared tray, smooth the top with a damp palette knife and let cool. Chill, uncovered, in the refrigerator until 30 minutes before finishing.

To make the mojo, put the shallots and lime zest and juice in a bowl, stir gently, then gradually stir in the oil, papaya and salt and pepper to taste. Remove the coriander leaves from the stalks, then add to the mojo with the chives. Fold the mojo into the beans.

Carefully take the polenta out of the tray and transfer to a chopping board. Cut into 12 wedges. Heat a ridged stove-top grill pan and, when it starts to smoke, lower the heat a little, spray with olive oil and add the polenta. Grill on the 'top' side for 2 minutes, then turn the pieces 180 degrees to create a charred criss-cross pattern. Cook for 1 minute more. Serve hot with the papaya mojo and beans.

Melon works well in salads alongside salty ingredients such as the feta cheese used here. The sugar snap peas add a delicious crunch to the melting texture of the melon and the crumbly feta. Savory is a herb with a spicy, peppery taste that is good with beans, including edamame (fresh soy beans). If you can't find savory, you could use thyme instead.

FETA SALAD
with watermelon

200 g edamame (fresh soy beans)
200 g broad beans, shelled
150 g sugar snap peas
½ small watermelon
4 tablespoons sunflower oil
200 g feta cheese
young leaves from 5 sprigs of savory
freshly ground black pepper

serves 6

Bring a large saucepan of unsalted water to the boil. Add the edamame and broad beans and blanch for 2 minutes. Drain, refresh under cold running water, then drain again. Remove the edamame from their pods and the broad beans from their skins. Transfer to a large serving bowl.

Blanch the sugar snap peas in boiling salted water for 30 seconds. Drain, refresh under cold running water, then drain again. Slice the sugar snaps lengthways. Add to the serving bowl with the edamame and broad beans.

Peel and slice the watermelon over a bowl to catch the juices. Cut the watermelon into small wedges. Squeeze a few pieces of melon over a small bowl to get about 3 tablespoons of juice. Add the remaining melon wedges to the beans. Whisk the oil into the watermelon juice and pour it over the salad.

Crumble the feta over the top, sprinkle with young savory leaves and pepper, then serve.

In Sicily, the land of orange and lemon groves, this salad is often served after grilled fish – especially in the region around Palermo. It is an example of the Sicilians' passion for sweet and savoury combinations and it is very refreshing.

ORANGE, ENDIVE AND BLACK OLIVE SALAD

2 oranges

1 red onion

125 g curly endive or escarole

DRESSING

finely grated zest and juice of 1 unwaxed orange

6 tablespoons extra virgin olive oil

2 tablespoons thinly sliced fresh basil leaves

2 tablespoons finely chopped, pitted, Greek-style, oven-dried black olives

2 sun-dried tomatoes in oil, drained and finely chopped

sea salt and freshly ground black pepper

serves 4

To make the dressing, put the orange zest and juice, olive oil, basil, olives and sun-dried tomatoes in a large bowl. Mix well, season with salt and pepper and set aside to develop the flavours.

Peel the oranges with a sharp knife, removing all the skin and white pith. Cut out the segments, put in a bowl and set aside. Slice the onion thinly using a very sharp thin-bladed knife or a mandolin. Immediately toss the onion and oranges in the dressing, then let marinate in a cool place for 15 minutes.

Put the endive on a plate and pile the dressed orange and onion mixture in the centre. Spoon over any remaining dressing and serve immediately.

Papaya grows everywhere in Thailand and is widely available. Young, unripened papaya is a basic salad ingredient in street food stalls, where it is pounded with fresh, spicy ingredients into a cold dish to accompany others. Now this staple dish has found great popularity in the West as the basis of a cold salad mixed with more expensive seafood such as lobster, crab, prawns or squid.

PAPAYA SALAD
with squid

500 g squid, cleaned, with tentacles separated

4 garlic cloves, peeled

3–4 small fresh red or green chillies

4 Chinese long beans, chopped into 5 cm lengths or 12 green beans, trimmed and halved

500 g fresh green papaya, peeled, deseeded and cut into thin slivers

2 tomatoes, cut into wedges

4 tablespoons Thai fish sauce

2 tablespoons sugar

4 tablespoons freshly squeezed lime juice

TO SERVE

a selection of fresh firm green vegetables in season, such as iceberg lettuce, cucumber or white cabbage

lime wedges

serves 4

To prepare the squid tubes, slit down both sides of the tubes and open out. Put on a board soft side up, then lightly run your knife diagonally, both ways, without cutting all the way through, making diamond patterns (this makes the squid cook evenly and curl up attractively). Alternatively, just cut the tubes into slices.

Put 600 ml water in a saucepan, bring to the boil, add the squid and simmer for 3 minutes. Drain and set aside.

Using a large mortar and pestle, pound the garlic to a paste, then add the chillies and pound again. Add the long beans, breaking them up slightly. Stir in the papaya with a spoon. Lightly pound together, then stir in the tomatoes and lightly pound again. Add the squid and mix well.

Stir in the fish sauce, sugar and lime juice, then transfer to a serving dish. Serve with fresh raw vegetables and lime wedges, using any leaves as a scoop for the spicy mixture.

The beef in this recipe is char-grilled but very rare. If you don't like rare meat, substitute something else, don't cook the meat until it's well done or even medium. Crispy roasted duck legs, poached chicken or prawns all work well. The mango, with its juicy sweetness, contrasts perfectly with the fiery chillies. Papaya is a good alternative.

THAI MANGO BEEF SALAD

4 bundles of beanthread vermicelli noodles, about 30 g each (optional)

2 tablespoons dark soy sauce

1 tablespoon Thai fish sauce

1 tablespoon brown sugar

500 g fillet of beef

4 small pink Thai shallots, or 2 regular, thinly sliced

1 mini cucumber* or 10 cm regular cucumber, thinly sliced

1 stalk of lemongrass, outer leaves removed and discarded, remainder very thinly sliced

DRESSING

4 tablespoons freshly squeezed lime juice

4 tablespoons Thai fish sauce

1 teaspoon brown sugar or palm sugar

TO SERVE

1 ripe mango, peeled and cut into 1 cm cubes

2 fresh red chillies, thinly sliced diagonally

2 spring onions, thinly sliced

a large handful of fresh mint leaves

serves 4

If serving with noodles, put them in a heatproof bowl and cover with hot water. Let soak for about 15 minutes, then drain. Transfer to a bowl of cold water until ready to serve, then drain and cut into short lengths, 5–10 cm long, with kitchen scissors.

Put the soy, fish sauce and sugar in a large, shallow bowl and beat with a fork to dissolve the sugar. Add the beef and turn to coat. Set aside for 1–2 hours to develop the flavours. Preheat a barbecue or stove-top grill pan until very hot, then cook the beef, turning from time to time, until the outside is well browned and the middle still pink, about 5 minutes in total, depending on the thickness of the meat. Remove the beef from the heat and set aside in a warm place for about 5 minutes to set the juices.

Put the meat on a board and slice thinly crossways. Cut the slices into bite-sized strips about 5 cm long.

To make the dressing, put the lime juice, fish sauce and sugar in a large bowl and beat with a fork to dissolve the sugar. Add the beef slices and any meat juices, the shallots, cucumber and lemongrass. Toss well.

Put a pile of noodles, if using, onto each plate, then top with the dressed salad. Add the mango, chillies and spring onions, then spoon any remaining dressing from the bowl over each serving. Top with mint leaves and serve.

*NOTE Mini or 'Lebanese' cucumbers aren't as watery as the regular kind. If you can't get them, use part of an ordinary one, but cut it in half lengthways and scrape out the seeds before slicing.

MAINS

Who says sweet and savoury flavours don't work together? The sweet accent of fruit can add a depth of flavour to many savoury dishes. Whether you're cooking fish, chicken or meat, fruit can play a delicious part. Duck can be enlivened with plums, while pork is taken to new heights with a delicious apple and blackberry compote. Lamb is transformed into a rich Armenian stew with pomegranates and apples and red mullet is given a citrus tang with the addition of blood oranges.

The rose and gold skin of the red mullet looks beautiful with the deep red of the blood oranges. If you can't find this fish, try red snapper and regular oranges instead. Citrus fruits are often cooked with fish in Italy – their gentle acidity brings out the sweetness of the flesh. These are cooked without wine, but you could add a tablespoon to each serving if tempted. The aroma when you open the parcel is wonderful.

RED MULLET AND BLOOD ORANGES COOKED IN A PARCEL

2 unwaxed oranges, preferably tarocchi or blood oranges

2 tablespoons extra virgin olive oil, plus extra for brushing

8 fresh bay leaves

4 red mullet or small red snapper, 250 g each, carefully scaled, cleaned and filleted

20 small black olives

sea salt and freshly ground black pepper

foil or baking parchment

a baking sheet

serves 4

Cut 4 rectangles of foil or baking parchment large enough to wrap each fish loosely. Brush with a little oil.

Grate the zest from the oranges into a bowl, then mix in the olive oil and salt and pepper to taste. Set aside. Peel the oranges as you would an apple, removing all the white pith, then slice the flesh thinly. Put 1 bay leaf in the cavity of each fish and 1 on top. Put a pile of orange slices on one side of each parchment or foil square, using half the orange slices in total. Put the fish on top of the oranges and cover them with the remaining orange slices. Sprinkle with the oil and orange zest mixture, then add the olives. Season well with salt and pepper.

If you have a water sprayer, lightly spritz the inside of the baking parchment. Fold the paper loosely over the fish and twist the edges together. Lift the parcels onto the baking sheet and bake in a preheated oven at 190°C (375°F) Gas 5 for 20 minutes.

Serve the parcels on warm plates, letting guests open their own parcels at the table.

Brining is usually associated with pickling, but when used for meat or poultry, think of it more as a marinade. It does not necessarily make things salty – it mostly intensifies the flavour and tenderizes the flesh to perfection. The roasted lemons add a bracing sour-sweetness, making this an innocent-looking, but deliciously potent combination.

TENDER BRINED CHICKEN
with honey-thyme roasted lemons

280 g coarse salt

75 g sugar

1 bay leaf

1 lemon, quartered

7–8 peppercorns

*1 organic or corn-fed chicken,
1.5 kg, trussed*

1–2 tablespoons extra virgin olive oil

HONEY-THYME ROASTED LEMONS

3–4 large lemons, halved

4 teaspoons honey

a small bunch of thyme sprigs

fine sea salt

kitchen foil

serves 4

Put the salt and sugar in a large mixing bowl. Add 2 litres cold water and stir until the salt has dissolved. Add the bay leaf, 1 lemon quarter and the peppercorns. Put the chicken in a deep, non-reactive, lidded pot and pour over the brine mixture. Chill for 2–8 hours.

To prepare the lemon halves, trim them at the base so they will sit flat. Arrange on a large sheet of foil (just off-centre so that you can fold the larger side over to enclose). Sprinkle each half with a good pinch of salt, then trickle about ½ teaspoon honey over each one. Top with 2–3 thyme sprigs. Fold over the foil and seal well.

Remove the chicken from the brine and rinse very well; don't leave any salt or it will be inedible (and don't add any salt either). Pat thoroughly dry – a soggy chicken won't roast properly. Stuff the remaining lemon quarters inside the chicken. Rub the outside with 1–2 tablespoons oil and set on a roasting rack, on its side. Put the chicken and parcel of lemons in a preheated oven at 200°C (400°F) Gas 6 and roast until the chicken juices run clear when the thigh is pierced with a knife, 50–60 minutes. Turn the chicken on its other side halfway through cooking.

Let rest for 15 minutes, then carve. Open the lemon parcel carefully; it will have lovely juices inside that you don't want to lose. Serve the chicken immediately, with the lemons and their juices alongside.

NOTE Don't roast the lemons in the pan with the chicken. The honey burns and fills the oven with smoke. If oven space is a problem, roast the lemons first and leave them wrapped and unopened until ready to serve; they don't have to be hot.

1 teaspoon ground saffron

2 cm piece of fresh ginger, peeled and grated

1½ tablespoons paprika

1 teaspoon freshly ground black pepper

2 teaspoons ground cinnamon

1 chicken, cut into 8 pieces

125 ml olive oil

2 large onions, grated

a pinch of saffron threads, soaked in boiling water for 30 minutes

6 garlic cloves, crushed

2 cinnamon sticks, broken in half

6 cloves

10 cardamom pods, lightly crushed

2 quinces, cored and cut into wedges

2 preserved lemons (optional)

coriander leaves, to serve

serves 4

A tagine is the Moroccan clay cooking pot with a conical lid, and also any dish cooked in it. The shape encourages steam to rise into the lid, then drop back onto the meat, keeping it moist. Tagines often include fruits of various kinds, but the elegant, scented quince is a favourite in Morocco in the autumn. When unavailable, slightly unripe pears can be used instead, as they belong to the same botanical family. Preserved lemons add a salty tang: you can buy them in Middle Eastern food stores.

CHICKEN TAGINE
with quinces and preserved lemons

Put the ground saffron, ginger, paprika, pepper and ground cinnamon in a bowl and mix well. Rub the chicken pieces with the mixture, put in a bowl, cover with clingfilm and let marinate for at least 30 minutes or overnight in the refrigerator.

Heat the olive oil in a heavy-based casserole. Add the chicken and fry on all sides until golden. Add the onion, then the saffron threads and their soaking liquid, the garlic, cinnamon sticks, cloves and cardamom pods. Add 125 ml water and bring to the boil on top of the stove. Cover and simmer on top of the stove or in a preheated oven at 150°C (300°F) Gas 2 for 45 minutes, or until part-cooked.

Peel the quince wedges, add to the tagine and continue cooking for 30 minutes or until the chicken is done and the quinces are tender.

If using preserved lemons, cut them into quarters and scrape off and discard the flesh. Cut the peel into thick slices lengthways, stir into the tagine and heat through for 5–10 minutes. Serve the tagine sprinkled with coriander leaves.

Duck breasts make a quick and easy dish. Cook them on a stove-top grill pan or in a heavy-based frying pan. The skin will turn very black and crispy from the sugar, and the rich flesh is balanced perfectly by the sweetness of spiced plums.

DUCK WITH SPICED PLUMS

4 duck breasts, with skin, about 200 g each

1 tablespoon honey

1 tablespoon dark soy sauce

25 ml rice wine vinegar

25 g palm sugar or soft brown sugar

¼ teaspoon ground cinnamon

4 plums, halved and stoned

sea salt and freshly ground black pepper

a stove-top grill pan (optional)

serves 4

Using a sharp knife, cut several slashes in the duck skin. Rub the skin with salt and pepper. Put the honey and soy sauce in a shallow dish, stir well, add the duck breasts and let marinate for at least 15 minutes.

Put the vinegar, sugar, cinnamon and 2 tablespoons water in a saucepan and heat until the sugar dissolves. Bring to the boil, add the plums and simmer gently for 8–10 minutes until the plums have softened. Let cool.

Meanwhile, heat a stove-top grill pan or heavy-based frying pan until hot, add the duck skin side down and cook over medium heat for 5 minutes. Turn and cook for a further 4–5 minutes, then remove from the heat and let rest in a low oven for 5 minutes.

Slice the duck crossways and serve with the plums and a little of the spiced juice.

4 duck breasts, about 200 g each

Asian salad leaves, to serve

THAI SPICE MARINADE

2 stalks of lemongrass

6 kaffir lime leaves

2 garlic cloves, coarsely chopped

2 cm piece of fresh ginger, coarsely chopped

4 coriander roots, washed and dried

2 small fresh red chillies, deseeded and coarsely chopped

200 ml extra virgin olive oil

2 tablespoons sesame oil

2 tablespoons Thai fish sauce

MANGO AND SESAME SALSA

1 large ripe mango, peeled, stoned and chopped

4 spring onions, chopped

1 fresh red chilli, deseeded and chopped

1 garlic clove, crushed

1 tablespoon light soy sauce

1 tablespoon freshly squeezed lime juice

1 teaspoon sesame oil

½ tablespoon sugar

1 tablespoon chopped fresh coriander

sea salt and freshly ground black pepper

TEA-SMOKE MIXTURE

8 tablespoons soft brown sugar

8 tablespoons long grain rice

8 tablespoons tea leaves

2 cinnamon sticks, bruised

1 star anise

The tea-smoke mixture adds a lovely spicy aroma to the duck. Cook the duck with the skin on, but remove it after cooking, if preferred. You will need a barbecue with a lid. If you have a gas barbecue, follow the manufacturer's instructions for indirect grilling and smoking.

TEA-SMOKED ASIAN SPICED DUCK BREAST
with mango and sesame salsa

To make the Thai spice marinade, use a sharp knife to trim the lemongrass stalks to 15 cm, then remove and discard the tough outer layers. Chop the inner stalks coarsely. Put them in a mortar, add the lime leaves, garlic, ginger, coriander roots and chillies and pound with a pestle to release the aromas. Transfer the mixture to a bowl, add the oils and fish sauce and set aside to infuse until required.

Using a sharp knife, cut several slashes into the duck skin, then put the duck in a shallow dish. Add the marinade, cover and let marinate in the refrigerator overnight. Remove from the refrigerator 1 hour before cooking.

Meanwhile, to make the salsa, put the chopped mango in a bowl, then add the spring onions, chilli, garlic, soy sauce, lime juice, sesame oil, sugar, coriander, salt and pepper. Mix well and set aside for 30 minutes to let the flavours infuse.

Preheat the barbecue. When the coals are hot, rake them into two piles at either side of the grill and put a foil drip tray in the middle.

Put all the ingredients for the tea-smoke mixture in a bowl and mix well. Transfer to a sheet of foil, fold the edges over and around the smoke mixture, seal well, then pierce the foil in about 10 places. Put the foil parcel directly on top of the hot coals, cover with the barbecue lid and wait until smoke appears. Remove the duck from the marinade and put onto the grill rack over the drip tray. Cover with the lid and cook for 15 minutes until the duck is cooked through. Discard the marinade.

Let the duck rest briefly, then serve with the mango and sesame salsa and some Asian salad leaves.

serves 4

4 tablespoons olive oil

750 g lamb neck fillets or boneless leg of lamb, cut into 2 cm chunks

2 large onions, chopped

2 garlic cloves, crushed

2 sweet red ramiro peppers, deseeded and chopped

4 ripe tomatoes, skinned, deseeded and coarsely chopped

½ teaspoon cayenne pepper

250 ml fresh vegetable stock or water

10 prunes

10 dried apricots

100 g okra, trimmed

2 Granny Smith apples, peeled, cored and cubed

400 g canned chickpeas, drained and rinsed

1 pomegranate, cut in half

a bunch of basil

a bunch of coriander

sea salt and freshly ground black pepper

a large ovenproof casserole

serves 6–8

This is a version of bozbash, an Armenian rich lamb stew, packed with herbs and fruity delicious flavours and textures. Neck fillet cooks quickly to tenderness owing to the small amount of fat running through it, so ideally use that. Pomegranates are a typical ingredient in this part of the world – sweet yet tart, with glorious colour, but leave them out if they're not in season. The herbs must be added at the last moment to keep their aromatic freshness.

FRUITY LAMB STEW
with basil and coriander

Heat a large flameproof casserole over high heat, add 2 tablespoons of the oil, then add the lamb in batches and brown on all sides. Remove to a plate, add 1 tablespoon oil to the casserole, then add the onions, garlic and red peppers and fry gently over low heat for 10 minutes.

Increase the heat and add the tomatoes and cayenne pepper and cook until bubbling, about 5 minutes. Add the browned lamb, the stock or water, salt and pepper and bring to a gentle simmer. Cover with a lid and cook in a preheated oven at 200°C (400°F) Gas 6 for 20–30 minutes until just softening. Add the prunes and apricots and cook for a further 10 minutes.

Heat the remaining 1 tablespoon oil in a frying pan, add the okra and apples and fry for 5 minutes. Transfer the okra, apples and chickpeas to the casserole and cook for a further 10 minutes. Test the meat for tenderness. If not yet done, lower the oven to 180°C (350°F) Gas 4 and cook for a further 10 minutes. Just before serving, squeeze the juice from half the pomegranate and fold into the casserole. Coarsely chop the herbs and fold half into the stew. Serve sprinkled with the remaining herbs and the seeds from the remaining pomegranate half.

½ teaspoon ground turmeric

½ teaspoon ground ginger

1 kg boned shoulder of lamb, trimmed of fat and cut into large chunks

25 g unsalted butter

2 onions, chopped

½ cinnamon stick

1 tomato, skinned and chopped, or 2 tablespoons chopped canned tomatoes

1 teaspoon honey (optional)

175 g dried apricots, halved

sea salt

RAS EL HANOUT

1 teaspoon cardamom seeds (not pods)

1 blade of mace or ½ teaspoon ground mace (optional)

1 teaspoon cubeb (optional) or peppercorns

3 allspice berries

½ cinnamon stick

a large pinch of saffron threads

1 teaspoon freshly grated nutmeg

1 teaspoon ground ginger

2–3 unsprayed dried rosebuds, torn into small pieces

TO SERVE

steamed couscous

a handful of coriander leaves

2 tablespoons sesame seeds, toasted in a dry frying pan

1–2 tablespoons argan oil (optional)*

Used in North African cooking, ras el hanout is an intricate spice blend, and it is all the more alluring for its mystery. If you can find cold-pressed argan oil, it gives the tagine a nutty finishing touch.

LAMB AND APRICOT TAGINE

To make the ras el hanout, toast the whole spices in a dry frying pan over low heat until aromatic. Stir in the nutmeg, ginger and rose petals. Just before using, grind the mixture to a powder with a mortar and pestle. (You will need only 1 tablespoon of the mixture for this recipe; store the remainder in an airtight container).

A few hours before making the tagine, put the turmeric and ginger in a bowl, mix well, then rub into the lamb. Cover and set aside to develop the flavours.

Melt the butter in a heavy-based saucepan or flameproof casserole and add the onions, cinnamon stick, lamb, 1 tablespoon ground ras el hanout and salt. Mix well, then add the chopped tomato, honey, if using, and 475 ml water. Bring to the boil, then reduce the heat to low and simmer gently, part-covered with a lid, for 45 minutes, stirring occasionally. Uncover and simmer for a further 45 minutes, stirring occasionally. Avoid the urge to raise the heat and cook the lamb quickly, as the slow simmering over low heat is responsible for the tagine's tenderness and for reducing the sauce to a rich coating.

Add the apricots and continue to simmer gently for 25 minutes. When ready, the sauce should just coat the lamb all over, rich and almost glaze-like. Remove the pan from the heat. Serve hot with couscous and sprinkle with coriander leaves, toasted sesame seeds and a little argan oil, if using.

*NOTE Argan oil is extracted from the nuts of Morocco's argan tree, and is said to be even healthier than the best olive oil. It is used in dips, on its own or in dressings. It is sometimes available in specialist shops and is definitely worth trying if you see it for sale.

serves 4

Inspired by some leftover fruit compote, this classic fruit combination is served simply with some pork chops. Fry the meat over medium heat so you don't burn the wonderful pan juices, which you then pour over the finished dish.

PORK STEAKS
with apple and blackberry compote

4 large pork steaks, about 250 g each

50 g butter

12 large fresh sage leaves

sea salt and freshly ground black pepper

APPLE AND BLACKBERRY COMPOTE

250 g cooking apples, cored and cut into thin wedges

75 g blackberries

2 tablespoons sugar

freshly squeezed juice of ½ lemon

3 juniper berries

serves 4

To make the compote, put the apples, blackberries, sugar, lemon juice, juniper berries and 2 tablespoons water in a saucepan. Cover the pan and cook gently until the fruits have softened. Remove the lid and simmer until the juices have evaporated. Remove the pan from the heat, but cover to keep the compote warm.

Season the pork steaks with salt and pepper. Melt the butter in a large frying pan and, as soon as it stops foaming, add the pork. Cook over medium heat for 3–4 minutes on each side until browned and cooked through.

Transfer the steaks to a plate and let rest in a warm oven for 5 minutes. Meanwhile, add the sage leaves to the hot frying pan and fry for a few seconds until crispy. Serve the steaks with a spoonful of the compote, the sage leaves and the pan juices poured over.

Pork and apple is a delicious combination. These mini pies are easily transportable and make a wonderful picnic dish.

MINI PORK AND APPLE PIES

250 g pork fillet, diced

125 g pork belly, diced

75 g smoked bacon, diced

25 g chicken livers

1 small onion, minced

1 tablespoon chopped fresh sage leaves

1 small garlic clove, crushed

a pinch of ground mace or nutmeg

1 red apple, peeled, cored and diced

sea salt and freshly ground black pepper

a green salad, to serve

PASTRY

300 g plain flour, plus extra for dusting

1½ teaspoons salt

60 g white vegetable fat

GLAZE

1 egg yolk

1 tablespoon milk

1 jam jar

6 pieces of wax paper, about 30 x 7 cm each

a baking sheet

serves 6

Put the pork fillet, pork belly, bacon and chicken livers in a food processor and blend briefly to mince the meat. Transfer to a bowl and mix in the onion, sage, garlic, mace or nutmeg and a little salt and pepper. Set aside.

To make the pastry, sift the flour and salt into a bowl. Put the fat and 150 ml water in a saucepan and heat gently until the fat melts and the water comes to the boil. Pour the liquid into the flour and, using a wooden spoon, gently draw the flour into the liquid to form a soft dough. Let cool for a few minutes and, as soon as the dough is cool enough to handle, knead lightly in the bowl until smooth.

Divide the dough into 8 equal pieces and roll out 6 of these on a lightly floured work surface to form circles 12 cm across. Carefully invert them, one at a time over an upturned jam jar. Wrap a piece of waxed paper around the outside, then tie around the middle with kitchen string.

Turn the whole thing over so the pastry is sitting flat. Carefully work the jar up and out of the pastry shell (you may need to slip a small palette knife down between the pastry and the jar to loosen it).

Divide the pork filling into 6 portions and put 1 portion in each pastry shell. Put the diced apple on top. Roll out the remaining 2 pieces of dough and, using a pastry cutter, cut 3 rounds from each piece the same size as the top of the pies.

Put a pastry round on top of each pie, press the edges together to seal, then turn the edges inwards and over to form a rim.

To make the glaze, put the egg yolk and milk in a bowl, beat well, then brush over the tops of the pies. Pierce each one with a fork to let the steam escape. Transfer to a large baking sheet and cook in a preheated oven at 190°C (375°F) Gas 5 for 45–50 minutes until golden. Remove from the oven, transfer to a wire rack, let cool and serve cold with a green salad.

PUDDINGS

Fruit is perfect for puddings. From fruit salads to tarts and pies, there are so many different ways to use fruit. Here you will find recipes for all types, from tropical varieties to berries and pears. There are ideas for raw fruit as well as baked and fried treats. Try a simple Strawberry and Mascarpone Trifle or, for the more adventurous, Lychee and Coconut Cheesecakes. There's a Classic Lemon Tart or Mango Cheeks with Spiced Palm Sugar Ice Cream. Whatever the season and whatever the occasion, there is something delicious here to inspire you.

Use any fruit that you can scoop out with a melon baller for this salad. Kaffir lime leaf, with its clean citrus flavours, is used to perfume the syrup. Pour the syrup over the fruit and churn the remainder into a soft sorbet. It seems like a lot of leaves, but it works. Buy them in big bags from Chinese or Asian markets, then use them fresh or freeze and use straight from frozen. Any leftovers may be used to make Thai curries.

SUMMER FRUIT SALAD
with kaffir lime sorbet

40 g kaffir lime leaves

225 g caster sugar

150 ml white wine, such as pinot grigio

1 egg white

1 orange-fleshed melon, such as Charentais or cantaloupe, halved and deseeded

1 green-fleshed melon, such as honeydew, halved and deseeded

1 small watermelon, preferably seedless, halved

2 ripe mangoes, cheeks removed

4 large kiwi fruit, peeled

1 dragon fruit*, peeled

an ice cream maker or large freezerproof container

melon ballers

serves 4–6

Tear the lime leaves and arrange in layers in a saucepan, sprinkling the sugar between the layers. Set aside for several hours or overnight to develop the flavours. Add 250 ml water to the pan and slowly heat to dissolve the sugar, then boil for 1 minute.

Strain the syrup and measure 200 ml into a bowl. Add the wine and 100 ml water and chill in the refrigerator. Set the remaining syrup aside until you are ready to make the salad.

Add the egg white to the chilled syrup and wine mixture and whisk just to break it up. Transfer to an ice cream maker and freeze according to the manufacturer's instructions. Eat immediately or store in the freezer. Alternatively, put the mixture in a large freezerproof container and freeze, stirring occasionally to break up the ice crystals.

When ready to serve, scoop balls of fruit into a bowl using one or several sizes of melon baller. Pour the reserved syrup over the top and keep cool until needed. Serve with scoops of the kaffir lime sorbet.

*NOTE Dragon fruit is a large pink tropical fruit covered with green and yellow horns. Its flesh is sweet, with tiny black seeds like vanilla. It is sold in Chinese and Asian markets, and sometimes in large supermarkets. If unavailable, use papaya instead.

'Dragon's eyes' is the romantic name for the longan fruit, a relative of the lychee, which you can use instead, either fresh or canned. Longans, which look like huge bunches of brown hairy grapes, are only available fresh in autumn, and you'll see special vendors selling them in Asian markets. Lemongrass and ginger are the distinctive flavours of Thailand. They make an easy syrup for this simple pudding to finish a Thai-style dinner and, like other Asian ingredients, are easy to use from frozen.

250 g caster sugar

2 cm piece of fresh ginger, peeled and thinly sliced

3 stalks of lemongrass, bruised and coarsely chopped

2 starfruit (carambola)

36 fresh longans or lychees, peeled and deseeded, or 2 cans, about 560 g each, drained

finely grated zest and juice of 1 unwaxed lime

2 baking sheets, lined with baking parchment

serves 6

LEMONGRASS-GINGER SYRUP with dragon's eyes

Put the sugar and 350 ml water in a heavy-based saucepan and heat gently to dissolve. Increase the heat, add the ginger and lemongrass and boil for 8 minutes until syrupy but still pale. Remove the pan from the heat and let cool completely.

To make the starfruit crisps, peel off the brown ridges of the starfruit with a vegetable peeler. Slice the fruit crossways very thinly using a mandolin. Arrange them on kitchen paper. Brush the top side with a little of the cold syrup and set them on the prepared baking sheets, painted side down. Lightly brush the top side with syrup. Cook in a preheated oven at 110°C (225°F) Gas ¼. Gently turn them over after 30 minutes, return to the oven and dry them out for a further 15 minutes. Carefully peel off the paper.

Strain the cooled syrup, leaving in a few bits of ginger. Add the longans or lychees, lime juice and zest to the cold syrup and chill until ready to serve with the starfruit crisps.

NOTE To test if the starfruit crisps are ready, take one out of the oven, it should crisp as it cools. They can be kept stored in an airtight container until ready to use. Apples can be cooked in the same way (there's no need to core or peel them).

SPONGE CAKE

225 g unsalted butter, softened

225 g caster sugar

4 large eggs, lightly beaten

50 g plain flour

275 g ground almonds

MINT SYRUP

30 g caster sugar

*12 fresh mint leaves,
finely chopped*

FILLING

about 500 g mascarpone cheese

25 g caster sugar

3 egg yolks

250 g raspberries

250 g strawberries

a small handful of fresh mint leaves

*a cake tin, 20 cm diameter, lined with
greaseproof paper*

1 large or 6 individual dishes

serves 6

A versatile pudding that is perfect for a warm, lazy day. Red fruit always looks magnificent but you could also use blueberries, mangoes and passion fruit. Only about half of the sponge is necessary for this trifle, so freeze the rest for an extra-speedy version next time round. The sponge has a dense, chewy texture to absorb the mint syrup. The mint is a perfect partner for the strawberries, but you could use fruit juice or sweet wine instead.

STRAWBERRY AND MASCARPONE TRIFLE

To make the sponge cake, put the butter and sugar in a medium bowl and beat with a hand-held electric mixer until pale and creamy. Gradually add the eggs, beating well after each addition. Using a metal spoon, fold in the flour and ground almonds. Spoon into the prepared cake tin and level the surface with a spatula. Bake in the centre of a preheated oven at 180°C (350°F) Gas 4 for 40 minutes until springy to the touch or until a skewer inserted into the centre comes out clean. Let cool in the tin for about 5 minutes, then invert onto a wire rack to cool completely.

To make the mint syrup, put the sugar, mint and 75 ml water in a small saucepan. Bring to the boil and continue to boil until reduced by one-third. Set aside.

To make the filling, put the mascarpone, sugar and egg yolks in a bowl and, using a hand-held electric mixer, beat until creamy. Using a fork, lightly mash the raspberries to a purée. Chop half the strawberries into small pieces, and cut the remainder in half, leaving the stalks intact for decoration.

To assemble the trifle, take half of the sponge cake and break it into large pieces (use the rest in another recipe). Put in the bottom of a large dish. Moisten the cake with the mint syrup and sprinkle with the mint leaves. Spoon in the raspberry purée, then the chopped strawberries, followed by the mascarpone mixture. Top with the halved strawberries. Chill in the refrigerator for 1 hour before serving.

This superb pudding doesn't have to be eaten solely in summer. A bag of frozen berries works just as well as the fresh fruit, so this delicious recipe can be enjoyed all year round.

SUMMER BRIOCHE PUDDING

4 small individual brioches

500 g fresh or frozen and thawed summer berries

4 tablespoons caster sugar

clotted cream or thick whipped cream, to serve

serves 4

Carefully trim the tops off the brioches and reserve as the lids. Using a small sharp knife, cut out a large cavity in the middle of each brioche.

Put the fruit and sugar in a saucepan and heat gently until the sugar has dissolved. Dip the brioche lids into the liquid, then spoon the fruit into the cavity. (It looks like a lot but the brioche will soak up all the fruit and juices.) Put the lids on top at a jaunty angle and chill in the refrigerator for at least 3 hours.

Serve with cream.

CRISPY OAT SCRUNCH

75 g plain or brown flour

75 g whole rolled oats

50 g unsalted butter

50 g demerara sugar

CREAM TOPPING

300 ml whipping cream

200 ml Greek yoghurt

35 g icing sugar or to taste

EXOTIC FRUIT LAYERS

2 medium papayas (about 500 g), peeled, deseeded and sliced

1 large mango (about 600 g), peeled, deseeded and sliced

2 fresh figs, quartered

4 passion fruit, halved

a baking sheet, 30 x 20 cm, greased

1 large or 4 individual glasses

serves 4

There are no limits to this pudding, which can be made with any fruits you like. The top can be decorated as extravagantly as you dare using grated or melted chocolate, lightly toasted desiccated coconut or flaked almonds, or a purée of sieved raspberries dribbled 'Jackson Pollock style' over the top! For anyone who feels guilty about puddings, take heart – the topping includes nearly as much yoghurt as cream.

EXOTIC FRUIT SCRUNCH

Put the flour and oats in a medium bowl and mix well. Using your fingertips, rub in the butter until the mixture resembles breadcrumbs. Stir in the demerara sugar, then press the mixture firmly onto the prepared sheet. Bake in a preheated oven at 200°C (400°F) Gas 6 for 15 minutes until lightly golden. Let cool, then break it up into large random pieces.

To make the cream topping, whip the cream until soft peaks form. Stir in the yoghurt and icing sugar, to taste.

Put the pieces of the oat scrunch in the bottom of 1 large glass serving bowl or 4 individual glasses, top with the papayas and mango, then the cream and yoghurt mixture and the figs. Scoop the passionfruit flesh over the top and serve.

BASE

150 g ginger biscuits

75 g butter

75 g caster sugar

FILLING

75 g creamed coconut block

75 ml sweet dessert wine, such as
Moscatel de Valencia

3 tablespoons stem ginger syrup

2 teaspoons powdered gelatine

24 fresh or canned lychees

5 tablespoons coconut liqueur,
such as Malibu

300 ml mascarpone cheese

3 tablespoons chopped
stem ginger

2 egg whites

50 g caster sugar

TO DECORATE

thinly sliced kiwi fruit

toasted shaved coconut

shredded stem ginger

6 loose-based tartlet tins,
about 10 cm diameter

serves 6

The subtle combination of coconut and lychee makes these individual cheesecakes irresistible. Creamed coconut comes in a solid block and has a good strong flavour – other types of coconut cream and milk will not give the same effect.

LYCHEE AND COCONUT CHEESECAKES

To make the crumb base, put the biscuits in a food processor and blend until crumbs form. Alternatively, put the biscuits in a plastic bag and crush finely with a rolling pin. Melt the butter and sugar in a small saucepan over gentle heat, then stir in the biscuit crumbs.

Press the crumb mixture into the bases and sides of the tart tins, then chill in the refrigerator until required.

Grate the creamed coconut and put in a saucepan with the sweet wine, ginger syrup and gelatine. Heat very gently until the coconut has melted. Do not boil. Stir well and pour into a blender.

Peel the fresh lychees, if using, and cut in half to remove the stones. Add either the fresh or canned lychees to the blender with the coconut liqueur and blend until smooth.

Put the mascarpone cheese in a large bowl and, using a wooden spoon or hand-held electric mixer, beat until softened. Gradually beat the lychee purée into the cheese, then stir in the stem ginger.

Put the egg whites in a spotlessly clean, grease-free bowl and whisk with a wire whisk or electric beaters until stiff but not dry. Whisk in the sugar, spoonful by spoonful, whisking until thick after each addition. Beat 2 spoonfuls of the meringue into the cheese mixture, then fold in the rest, using a large metal spoon. Pour the filling into the prepared tins and level the surface. Chill in the refrigerator for at least 30 minutes. Decorate with kiwi fruit slices, coconut shavings and shreds of stem ginger just before serving.

Serve this cheesecake as part of a buffet party. It is bursting with juicy pieces of tangerine, and is very refreshing after a meal. For a really special occasion, try using tangerines or clementines ready-prepared in a liqueur and sugar syrup, which are available from specialist grocery stores.

TANGERINE AND CHOCOLATE CHEESECAKE

BASE

100 g butter

225 g plain chocolate biscuits, crushed

FILLING

8 unwaxed tangerines

25 g powdered gelatine

450 g mascarpone or full-fat soft cheese

4 eggs, separated

175 g caster sugar

300 ml crème fraîche or sour cream

3 tablespoons Cointreau or Grand Marnier

TO DECORATE

swirls of cream

piped chocolate decorations

tangerine segments half-dipped in chocolate

a springform cake tin, 25 cm diameter, lined

serves 12

Put the butter in a small saucepan, melt over gentle heat, then stir in the biscuit crumbs. Press evenly into the base of the prepared cake tin and chill for 30 minutes.

Finely grate the zest of 2 tangerines and set aside. Squeeze the juice from 4 of the tangerines and pour into a small saucepan. Sprinkle with the gelatine and let sponge for 10 minutes. Remove the flesh from the segments of the remaining tangerines and chop coarsely.

Put the mascarpone in a large bowl and, using a wooden spoon or hand-held electric mixer, beat until softened. Beat in the egg yolks, 100 g of the caster sugar, the crème fraîche and liqueur. Heat the gelatine slowly until dissolved, then stir into the cheese mixture. Fold in the tangerine zest and chopped tangerines.

Put the egg whites in a spotlessly clean, grease-free bowl and beat with a wire whisk or electric beaters until stiff, then gradually whisk in the remaining caster sugar. Fold into the cheese mixture and spoon into the cake tin. Level the surface with a spatula and chill in the refrigerator for 3–4 hours until set.

Carefully remove the cheesecake from the tin onto a serving plate. Decorate with swirls of cream topped with a chocolate decoration and chocolate-dipped tangerine segments. Alternatively, pipe an irregular criss-cross pattern over the top of the cake with a little melted plain chocolate.

One of the easiest, quickest, and prettiest cakes you can make, this recipe is full of summer flavours. The all-in-one lemon sponge can be made from scratch in under an hour – the simple fruit topping takes just a couple of minutes to arrange.

CITRUS SUMMER CAKE

LEMON CURD

110 g unsalted butter

230 g caster sugar

the grated zest and juice of 2 large or 3 medium unwaxed lemons

3 large eggs, beaten

SPONGE

175 g unsalted butter, softened but not oily

250 g caster sugar

3 large eggs, at room temperature, beaten

250 g self-raising flour

½ teaspoon baking powder

125 ml milk

the grated zest of 2 medium unwaxed lemons

TOPPING

2 tablespoons toasted flaked almonds

250 g mixed berries (such as strawberries, raspberries, blueberries, blackberries and redcurrants)

icing sugar, for dusting

a daisy tin, a non-stick cake tin, 27 x 18 cm, or a roasting tin, greased

makes 1 cake

To make the lemon curd, put the butter, sugar and lemon zest and juice in the top of a non-aluminium double saucepan or in a saucepan set in a roasting tin of boiling water. Set the double pan or roasting tin over medium heat, so the water boils gently. Cook the butter mixture, stirring constantly with a wooden spoon, until smooth and melted. Add the eggs and stir until the mixture becomes very thick and opaque – avoid short cuts, because if the mixture boils, the eggs will scramble. Spoon into clean jars. When completely cold, use as needed or cover and store in the refrigerator for up to 2 weeks.

To make the sponge, put the butter, sugar, eggs, flour, baking powder, milk and lemon zest in an electric mixer. Using medium speed, beat until the mixture is thick and fluffy with no sign of lumps or streaks of flour.

Spoon the mixture into the prepared tin and spread evenly. Bake in a preheated oven at 180°C (350°F) Gas 4 for about 30 minutes, or until a skewer inserted in the centre comes out clean. Let cool in the tin for 10 minutes, then turn out onto a wire rack to cool completely. When cold, the cake can be stored in an airtight container for up to 2 days.

When ready to serve, set the cake on a serving platter. Brush the sides and top of the cake with about 4 tablespoons of the lemon curd, then sprinkle flaked almonds all over it. Arrange the berries on top and around the cake, dust with icing sugar and serve.

Store in an airtight container in the refrigerator and eat within 2 days.

A great stand-by when time is tight and you are cooking a special meal – you can choose your favourite fruit for this pudding, depending what is in season. Dessert blackberries plus a high fruit content blackberry conserve work well, though you could use raspberries, strawberries, blueberries, dark cherries (pitted), all with the matching conserves.

EASY CHOCOLATE AND BLACKBERRY ROULADE

110 g caster sugar

2 large eggs

50 g unsalted butter, very soft

100 g self-raising flour

3 tablespoons cocoa powder

1 teaspoon pure vanilla essence

2 tablespoons warm water

FILLING

4 tablespoons blackberry conserve

200 g crème fraîche

250 g blackberries

TO SERVE

icing sugar, for sprinkling

chocolate curls or freshly grated chocolate

a Swiss roll tin or baking sheet, about 20 x 30 cm, buttered and lined with baking parchment

serves 6–8

Put the sugar, eggs and butter in a mixing bowl, or the bowl of an electric mixer. Sift the flour and cocoa into the bowl, then add the vanilla essence and 2 tablespoons warm water. Whisk for about 1 minute or until you have a smooth, thick and creamy batter. Pour the mixture into the prepared tin and spread it evenly with a spatula.

Bake in a preheated oven at 200°C (400°F) Gas 6 for 8 minutes or until the mixture is well risen and just springy when you press it with your finger. Let cool in the tin for about 1 minute.

Meanwhile, put a sheet of baking parchment on a work surface and sprinkle heavily with icing sugar. Turn the sponge out onto the baking parchment, then peel off the lining paper. Carefully roll up the sponge with the parchment inside, like a Swiss roll. Cover with a damp tea towel and leave on the wire rack until completely cold.

Put the conserve and crème fraîche in a bowl and, using a metal spoon, fold gently together. Carefully unroll the sponge. Don't worry if it has cracked. Spread the cream mixture over the sponge, then sprinkle the berries evenly over the top.

Roll up the sponge fairly loosely and set on a large serving plate. Cover and chill until ready to serve – the texture can be better the next day, but it's best eaten within 48 hours. Just before serving, sprinkle with icing sugar and decorate with chocolate curls.

This classic tart is filled with an uncooked lemon curd and baked in the oven until just firm. You could make very tiny ones for special occasions – if you are making bite-sized morsels, the pastry must be wonderfully thin so that they melt in the mouth.

CLASSIC LEMON TART

1 egg, beaten, to seal the pastry

crème fraîche, to serve (optional)

SWEET RICH SHORTCRUST PASTRY

250 g plain flour, plus extra for dusting

½ teaspoon salt

2 tablespoons icing sugar

125 g unsalted butter, chilled and diced

2 egg yolks

2 tablespoons iced water

LEMON FILLING

6 large eggs

350 g caster sugar

finely grated zest and strained juice of 4 juicy unwaxed lemons

125 g unsalted butter, melted

a loose-based fluted tart tin, 23 cm diameter

kitchen foil, baking parchment or all-purpose clingfilm

baking beans

a baking sheet

serves 8

To make the pastry, sift the flour, salt and icing sugar into a bowl, then rub in the butter. Mix the egg yolks with the 2 tablespoons iced water. Add to the flour, mixing together lightly with a knife. The pastry must have some water in it or it will be too difficult to handle. If the pastry is too dry, add a little more water, sprinkling it over the flour mixture 1 tablespoon at a time. Turn the mixture out onto a lightly floured work surface. Knead lightly with your hands until smooth. Form the dough into a rough ball, flatten slightly, then wrap in clingfilm. Chill for at least 30 minutes before rolling out.

Bring the pastry to room temperature, then roll it out thinly on a lightly floured work surface, and use to line the tart tin. Chill or freeze for 15 minutes.

Line the pastry case with foil, baking parchment or all-purpose clingfilm (flicking the edges inwards towards the centre so that they don't catch on the pastry), then fill with baking beans. Set on a baking sheet and bake blind in the centre of a preheated oven at 190°C (375°F) Gas 5 for 10–12 minutes. Remove the foil, baking parchment or clingfilm and the baking beans and return the pastry case to the oven for a further 5–7 minutes to dry out completely. Brush with beaten egg, then bake again for 5–10 minutes until set and shiny to prevent the filling from making the pastry soggy. Remove from the oven and set aside.

Lower the oven to 150°C (300°F) Gas 2. To make the lemon filling, put the eggs, sugar, lemon zest and juice and butter in a food processor and blend until smooth.

Set the baked tart shell on a baking sheet and pour in the filling. Bake in the oven for about 1 hour (it may need a little longer, depending on your oven) until just set. Remove from the oven and let cool completely before serving.

Serve at room temperature, maybe with a spoonful of crème fraîche.

Golden Delicious is the apple of preference for this French tart. It's not an especially interesting eating variety, but it's perfect for baking and cooking. It holds its shape well and is not too tart. The vanilla-scented purée is an extra, but worth the indulgence.

SIMPLE APPLE TART

PASTRY

200 g plain flour, plus extra for dusting

2 teaspoons caster sugar

100 g cold unsalted butter, cut into pieces

a pinch of salt

APPLE PURÉE

3 Golden Delicious apples, peeled and chopped

1 vanilla pod, split lengthways with a small sharp knife

2 tablespoons sugar

10 g unsalted butter

APPLE TOPPING

3 Golden Delicious apples, peeled and sliced

15 g unsalted butter, melted

1 tablespoon sugar

a loose-based tart tin, 27 cm diameter, greased and floured

baking parchment and baking beans or baking weights

serves 6

To make the pastry, put the flour, sugar, butter and salt in a food processor and, using the pulse button, process until the butter is broken down (5–10 pulses). Add 3 tablespoons cold water and pulse just until the dough forms coarse crumbs; add 1 more tablespoon water if necessary, but do not do more than 10 pulses.

Transfer the pastry to a sheet of baking parchment, form into a ball and flatten to a disc. Wrap in the parchment and chill in the refrigerator for 30–60 minutes.

Roll out the pastry on a lightly floured work surface to a disc slightly larger than the tart tin. Carefully transfer the pastry to the tin, patching any holes as you go and pressing gently into the sides. To trim the edges, roll a rolling pin over the top, using the edge of the tin as a cutting surface, and letting the excess fall away. Tidy up the edges and chill in the refrigerator until firm, 30–60 minutes.

Prick the pastry all over with a fork, line with the parchment and fill with baking beans or baking weights. Bake in a preheated oven at 200°C (400°F) Gas 6 for 15 minutes, then remove the parchment and weights and bake until just golden, 10–15 minutes more. Let the tart shell cool slightly before filling.

To make the apple purée, put the chopped apples, vanilla pod, sugar and butter in a saucepan, add 4 tablespoons water and cook gently, stirring often until soft, adding more water if necessary, 10–15 minutes. Use the tip of a small knife to scrape the seeds out of the vanilla pod into the purée, then discard the pod. Transfer the mixture to a food processor, blender or food mill and purée.

Spread the purée evenly in the pastry case. Arrange the apple slices in a circle around the edge; they should be slightly overlapping but not completely squashed together. Repeat for an inner circle, trimming the slices slightly so they fit, and going in the opposite direction from the outer circle. Brush with the melted butter and sprinkle with the sugar. Bake in a preheated oven at 200°C (400°F) Gas 6 until just browned and tender, 25–35 minutes. Serve warm or at room temperature.

A classic of the French pâtisserie – thin crisp pastry filled with a thin layer of golden custard and topped with soft, musky apricots, glistening with apricot jam and their edges just 'caught' in the oven. The pastry case is not baked blind because it would burn.

APRICOT TART

1 recipe Pâte Sucrée (page 114)

flour, for dusting

CRÈME PÂTISSIÈRE

5 egg yolks

75 g caster sugar

3 tablespoons plain flour

400 ml milk

2 tablespoons kirsch or brandy

APRICOT TOPPING AND GLAZE

500–600 g fresh apricots, depending on their size

50 g caster sugar

3 tablespoons apricot jam

a little kirsch or brandy

a loose-based tart tin, 25 cm diameter

a non-stick baking sheet with a rim

a regular baking sheet

a wire rack

serves 6–8

Bring the pâte sucrée to room temperature before rolling out.

To make the crème pâtissière, put the egg yolks and sugar in a bowl and beat with a wooden spoon or electric beaters until pale and thick. Beat in the flour. Put the milk in a small saucepan and bring to the boil, then whisk into the egg mixture. Return the mixture to the pan and bring to the boil again, stirring constantly. Cook gently for 2–3 minutes, then pour into a bowl and let cool, covering the surface with clingfilm to prevent a skin from forming.

Roll out the pâte sucrée on a lightly floured work surface and line the tart tin with it. Chill in the refrigerator for at least 30 minutes.

Cut the apricots in half and remove the pits. Arrange them cut side down on a baking sheet with a rim and sprinkle with sugar. Bake in a preheated oven at 230°C (450°F) Gas 8 (or as hot as the oven will go) for 5 minutes until softening and beginning to release their juices. Drain off and reserve the juices.

Lower the oven to 200°C (400°F) Gas 6 and put the regular baking sheet on the middle shelf to preheat. Beat the 2 tablespoons kirsch or brandy into the cooled crème pâtissière and spread over the base of the pastry case. Arrange the apricots closely together, cut side up, over the crème. Set the tart tin on the preheated baking sheet and bake for about 40 minutes until the apricots colour and the tart is a deep golden brown.* Remove from the oven and let cool for 10 minutes before lifting off the outer ring and transferring to a wire rack to cool completely.

Put the apricot jam in a small saucepan, add the reserved apricot juice and kirsch or brandy to taste and heat gently until liquid. Strain, then use to glaze the cooled tart. Serve at room temperature, preferably on the day of making.

*NOTE This tart is not baked blind, but setting the tart tin on a preheated baking sheet will help to ensure that the base cooks quickly and goes crisp.

Pudding and cheese in one. An original version of this tart used shortcrust pastry, blue cheese and pears. Here, puff pastry, figs and a triple-crème cheese are used, with thyme to add a delicious herbal note. Orange-scented thyme, if you can find it, would provide another interesting flavour.

FIG ON A CUSHION WITH THYME-SCENTED SYRUP

500 g puff pastry, thawed if frozen

flour, for dusting

6 sprigs of thyme, with flowers if available

75 g caster sugar

2 teaspoons grenadine (pomegranate syrup)

150–200 g triple-crème cheese, such as Saint André, cut horizontally to make 4 discs

6 fresh ripe figs, preferably purple, halved vertically

1 egg yolk, beaten with 2 teaspoons water

2 pastry cutters or templates, about 14 cm and 11 cm diameter

a baking sheet

serves 4

Put the pastry on a lightly floured work surface and roll out to about 28 cm square. Using the 14 cm pastry cutter or template, cut out 4 circles. Use the edge of the knife to 'knock up' or separate the layers of pastry horizontally so they will rise well. Set the circles on a baking sheet and chill in the refrigerator for 30 minutes.

Strip the leaves off 4 sprigs of thyme and put them in a small saucepan. Add the sugar and 75 ml water. Set over medium heat and slowly dissolve the sugar. Boil for 4 minutes. Remove from the heat, add the grenadine, let cool, then chill in the refrigerator.

Make slashes at 1 cm intervals around the edges of the pastry circles and score an inner circle to join up the slashes, or use the 11 cm pastry cutter – don't cut all the way through. Prick the inside of each inner circle with a fork.

Put 1 round of cheese in the middle of each pastry. Strip the leaves off the remaining 2 sprigs of thyme and sprinkle on top of the cheese. Arrange 3 fig halves on each piece of cheese.

Brush around the edges of the pastry with the beaten egg yolk, but don't let it drip down the sides or the tarts won't rise. Chill in the refrigerator until time to cook. Bake in a preheated oven at 220°C (425°F) Gas 7 for 20–25 minutes until puffed and golden. Strain the scented syrup, pour it over the figs, add a few pink thyme flowers, if using, then serve.

These exotic mouthfuls are very wicked. Remember, the more wrinkled the passion fruit, the riper the flesh inside. Why not make double the quantity of curd and pot up any you don't use?

PINEAPPLE AND PASSION FRUIT CURD TARTLETS

PÂTE SUCRÉE

200 g plain flour, plus extra for dusting

a pinch of salt

75 g caster or icing sugar

75 g unsalted butter, diced, at room temperature

2 egg yolks

½ teaspoon pure vanilla essence

2–3 tablespoons iced water

PASSION FRUIT CURD

6 ripe, juicy passion fruit

freshly squeezed juice of 1 small lemon, strained

75 g butter, cubed

3 large eggs, beaten

225 g sugar

FRUIT TOPPING

1 small fresh pineapple, peeled, cored and sliced

4 passion fruit

a fluted biscuit cutter, 7.5 cm diameter

a 12-hole bun tray

makes 12 tartlets

To make the pâte sucrée, sift the flour and salt onto a sheet of greaseproof paper. Put the sugar, butter, egg yolks and vanilla essence in a food processor, then blend until smooth. Add the water and blend again. Add the flour to the food processor and blend until just combined.

Transfer the dough to a lightly floured work surface and knead gently until smooth. Form into a flattened ball, then wrap in clingfilm. Chill in the refrigerator or freeze for at least 30 minutes. Bring the pastry to room temperature before rolling out.

Cut the 6 passion fruit in half, scoop out the flesh and press through a sieve into a medium bowl to extract the juice. Add the lemon juice, butter, eggs and sugar and set the bowl over a saucepan of simmering water (or cook in a double boiler). Cook, stirring all the time, for about 20 minutes or until the curd has thickened considerably. If you are brave enough, you can cook this over direct heat, watching that it doesn't get too hot and curdle. Strain into a bowl and set aside.

Roll out the pastry thinly on a lightly floured work surface and cut out 12 rounds with the biscuit cutter. Line the bun tray with the pastry, pressing it into the holes. Prick the bases and chill in the refreigerator or freeze for 15 minutes. Bake blind in a preheated oven at 180°C (350°F) Gas 4 for 5–6 minutes without lining the pastry with beans. Let cool.

When ready to serve, fill the tartlet cases with a spoonful of passion fruit curd, then top with slices of pineapple. Cut the 4 passion fruit in half, scoop out the flesh and spoon a little, seeds and all, over each tartlet. Serve immediately before the tartlets go soggy.

In Austria there is such a variety of strudels – all shapes and sizes, flavours and textures. This one is delicious. If fresh cherries are not available, use frozen ones, but drain them well before adding to the filling.

CURD CHEESE AND CHERRY STRUDELS

12 sheets Greek filo pastry (which tends to be thinner than most other types)

100 g butter, melted

icing sugar, for dusting

FILLING

60 g butter or margarine

60 g caster sugar

2 eggs, separated

250 g curd cheese, strained

finely grated zest of 1 unwaxed lemon

½ teaspoon ground cinnamon

60 ml sour cream

250 g fresh cherries, pitted and quartered

several large baking sheets, lightly greased

makes about 12

To make the filling, put the butter or margarine and sugar in a large bowl and, using a wooden spoon or hand-held electric mixer, beat until pale and fluffy. Stir in the egg yolks, strained curd cheese, lemon zest, cinnamon and sour cream, then fold in the cherries. Put the egg whites in a separate, spotlessly clean, grease-free bowl and, using a balloon whisk or hand-held electric mixer, whisk until stiff. Gently fold in the cheese mixture with a large metal spoon.

Keep the filo pastry sheets covered with clingfilm to prevent them from drying out. Put a filo sheet on a clean work surface and brush with a little of the melted butter. Starting at the short side of each sheet of pastry, 2.5 cm in from the front edge, spoon about 2 heaped tablespoons of the mixture along the edge, keeping 2.5 cm in from the sides. Flip the bottom edge over the filling, roll once, then flip the sides inwards to encase the filling completely. Roll up like a cigar, brush with melted butter and set on a large baking sheet. Repeat with the other sheets of pastry.

Bake in a preheated oven at 190°C (375°F) Gas 5 for about 20 minutes until the pastry is firm and golden brown. Remove from the oven and let cool slightly, then dust with icing sugar and serve warm.

NOTE If you make the filling in an electric blender, the curd cheese won't need to be strained.

Palm sugar adds the most wonderful toffee flavour to the ice cream, while star anise offers a hint of something more exotic. This, combined with warm mangoes provides a wickedly delicious pudding.

MANGO CHEEKS WITH SPICED PALM SUGAR ICE CREAM

3 large mangoes

icing sugar, for dusting

SPICED PALM SUGAR ICE CREAM

450 ml milk

300 ml double cream

75 g palm sugar, grated, or soft brown sugar

4 whole star anise

5 egg yolks

an ice cream maker or large freezerproof container

serves 4

To make the ice cream, put the milk, cream, sugar and star anise in a heavy-based saucepan and heat gently until the mixture just reaches boiling point. Set aside to infuse for 20 minutes. Put the egg yolks in a bowl and beat with a wooden spoon or hand-held electric mixer until pale. Stir in the infused milk. Return to the pan and heat gently, stirring constantly, until the mixture is thickened and coats the back of a spoon. Let cool completely, then strain.

Put the mixture in an ice cream maker and freeze according to the manufacturer's instructions. Alternatively, pour into a large freezerproof container and freeze for 1 hour until just frozen. Beat vigorously to break up the ice crystals and return to the freezer. Repeat several times until frozen. Soften in the refrigerator for 20 minutes before serving.

Using a sharp knife, cut the cheeks off each mango and put on a plate. Dust the cut side of each mango cheek with a little icing sugar. Preheat a barbecue or stove-top grill pan and grill the cheeks for 2 minutes on each side. Cut the cheeks in half lengthways and serve 3 wedges per person with the ice cream.

One of the best ways to cook pears is to bake them. This is so simple to make, but tastes luxurious. Choose pears that are ripe but not too soft, or they will overcook. If you can't find a good rich Marsala or Vin Santo, use sweet sherry or Madeira.

CARAMELIZED PEARS WITH MARSALA AND MASCARPONE CREAM

6 large ripe pears

150 g caster sugar

150 ml Marsala or Vin Santo

200 g mascarpone cheese

1 vanilla pod, split lengthways, seeds scraped out and reserved

a flameproof, ovenproof pan or dish

serves 6

Cut the pears in half and scoop out the cores – do not peel them. Sprinkle the sugar into the pan or dish. Set over medium heat and let the sugar melt and caramelize. Remove from the heat as soon as it reaches a medium-brown colour and quickly arrange the pears cut side down in the caramel.

Bake in a preheated oven at 190°C (375°F) Gas 5 until the pears are soft, 20–25 minutes. Carefully lift out the pears and transfer to an ovenproof serving dish, keeping the caramel in the pan.

Put the pan on top of the stove over medium heat and add the Marsala or Vin Santo. Bring to the boil, stirring to dislodge any set caramel, and boil fast until reduced and syrupy. Set aside.

Scoop out a good teaspoon of flesh from each cooked pear and put it in a bowl. Add the mascarpone and vanilla seeds and beat well. Fill the centres of the pears with the mascarpone mixture. Return to the preheated oven for 5 minutes until the mascarpone has heated through. Serve with the caramel sauce spooned over the top.

Clafoutis, a custard-like batter baked with whole cherries, is one of the finest French puddings and a cinch to make. The only drawback is that the cherry season is a short one, and it is a shame to limit clafoutis making to just one part of the year. Plums, pears and apples work well as substitutes, but rhubarb is fantastic. Almost better than the original.

RHUBARB CLAFOUTIS

500 g fresh rhubarb, cut into 3 cm slices

200 ml whole milk

200 ml double cream

3 eggs

150 g sugar

¼ teaspoon ground cinnamon

a pinch of salt

1 vanilla pod, split lengthways with a small sharp knife

50 g plain flour

icing sugar, for sprinkling (optional)

a large baking dish, about 30 cm diameter, greased with butter and sprinkled with sugar

serves 6

Bring a saucepan of water to the boil, add the rhubarb and cook for 2 minutes, just to blanch. Drain and set aside.

Put the milk, cream, eggs, sugar, cinnamon and salt in a bowl and mix well. Using the tip of a knife, scrape the vanilla seeds into the mixture. Add the flour and whisk well.

Arrange the rhubarb pieces in the prepared dish. Pour the batter over the top and bake in a preheated oven at 200°C (400°F) Gas 6 until puffed and golden, 40–45 minutes. Serve warm, sprinkled with icing sugar, if liked.

A Caribbean idea with its African roots in evidence. Sweet potatoes are great fritter vegetables, melting in your mouth with creamy sweetness. If you can find true plantains (platanos) at a shop selling exotic fruit and vegetables, snap them up – they, too, are perfect fritter material. Otherwise, under-ripe bananas will be convenient substitutes for plantains.

2 large sweet potatoes

2 under-ripe bananas or plantains

oil, for deep-frying

FROTHY BATTER

275 g plain flour

½ teaspoon freshly grated nutmeg

2 teaspoons ground cinnamon

about 425 ml sparkling water

TO SERVE

brown sugar or icing sugar

sweet salsa or chutney

serves 6–8 (makes about 38)

SWEET POTATO AND BANANA SPICED FRITTERS

To make the batter, put the flour, nutmeg and cinnamon in a large bowl and stir well. Make a well in the centre and gradually whisk in enough sparkling water to make a smooth batter, thick enough to coat the back of a spoon. The amount of water given here is a guide only. Cover with a tea towel and set aside for 20 minutes.

Cut the sweet potatoes into 1.5 cm slices, then cut in half (you should have about 28 half-moon pieces). Cut the bananas or plantains into 2.5 cm slices (about 10), because they will cook much faster.

Fill a deep saucepan one-third full of oil and heat to 190°C (375°F) or until a cube of bread browns in 30 seconds. Working in batches and using tongs, dip a piece of banana or plantain into the batter, coat well, then slide it into the hot oil – do not overcrowd the pan. Fry until golden brown all over. Remove with a slotted spoon, drain in a colander lined with kitchen paper, then transfer to a serving plate and keep them warm in a low oven while you cook the sweet potatoes, again in batches.

Sprinkle with sugar and serve hot. These fritters are great on their own, but you can also serve them with sweet salsa or chutney.

PRESERVES

There's nothing like the bounty of fresh fruit to inspire you to create some delicious homemade preserves. It is also wonderfully satisfying to stock your cupboards with your own jams and chutneys. Berries, rhubarb, apples and mangoes can all be used to make homely delights. To accompany freshly baked scones, there is a mouthwatering Strawberry Jam. Fill a Victoria sponge cake with your own Red Berry Jelly or spread some toast with some homemade Lemon, Lime and Grapefruit Marmalade. For a savoury note, try Apple, Plum or Indian Green Mango Chutney.

Strawberry has to be the all-time favourite fruit for jam. It is delicious served with freshly baked homemade scones, used in cakes and puddings or spread thickly on a slice of hot toast.

STRAWBERRY JAM

1 kg small strawberries, picked in dry weather

freshly squeezed juice of 1 lemon

1 kg sugar

4 clean, dry, warm jam jars (page 4), 250 g each, with lids or covers

waxed paper discs

makes about 1 kg

Wash the fruit if necessary and pat dry. Hull the strawberries and discard any that are not in perfect condition. Put in a large pan and cook gently over very low heat just for a few minutes to start the juices running. Take care not to let the fruit burn. Let stand overnight. If you like, the fruit can be mashed at this stage.

Add the lemon juice and sugar to the fruit and bring to simmering point over low heat. Stir well while the sugar is dissolving. When the sugar has dissolved, increase the heat and boil rapidly for 10 minutes (remember to stir occasionally to make sure the pan does not burn) until the juice has reduced and the jam starts to thicken.

Take the pan off the heat and test for set*. If the jam is not ready, put the pan back on the heat to boil for a few minutes longer and test again. Repeat this process if necessary and remember to take the jam off the heat while testing, because over-boiling will ruin it.

When setting point has been reached, skim the jam with a perforated skimmer, stir it well and let stand for 20 minutes for the fruit to settle. Stir and ladle into clean, dry, warm jars. Seal at once with waxed paper discs, wiping the necks of the jars with a clean, damp cloth if necessary. Close with a lid or appropriate cover.

Let cool, label and store in a cool, dark cupboard until required.

*NOTE To test for set, put a saucer and 2–3 teaspoons in the refrigerator or freezer to cool before you start making the jam. After boiling the jam hard for the specified time, take the pan off the heat. Put 1 teaspoon of the jam on the cold saucer in the refrigerator or freezer and leave for 5 minutes. Push it with a finger – if it offers resistance or crinkles, it is ready. If it is still liquid, return the pan to the heat, boil a few minutes longer and test again. Alternatively use a sugar thermometer to gauge setting point – 110°C (224°F).

This is a robust jam that deserves a place alongside the zingiest of marmalades. Choose young pink rhubarb if possible, because it will give a lovely pink colour to the jam – green rhubarb tends to turn brown when cooked. However, the flavour is just as good whatever the colour. This would also make a delicious old-fashioned pudding such as jam tart, Bakewell tart, jam roly-poly or steamed jam pudding.

RHUBARB AND GINGER JAM

1.5 kg young rhubarb, pink if possible

1.5 kg sugar

grated zest and freshly squeezed juice of 1½ unwaxed lemons

30–45 g fresh ginger, peeled, to taste

3–4 clean, dry, warm jam jars (page 4), 250 ml each, with lids or covers

waxed paper discs

makes about 1 kg

Wipe the rhubarb, trim it, cut into chunks and put in a bowl with the sugar, lemon zest and juice. Cover and let stand overnight.

Crush the ginger with a mortar and pestle or blender and add to the fruit and sugar. Transfer to a large saucepan and bring slowly to simmering point, stirring all the time to dissolve the sugar. Simmer gently until the fruit has softened, then increase the heat and boil rapidly for 5–10 minutes until setting point is reached (page 129).

If the jam is not ready, put the pan back on the heat to boil for a few minutes longer and test again. Repeat this process if necessary and remember to take the jam off the heat while testing, because over-boiling will ruin it.

When setting point has been reached, skim the jam with a perforated skimmer, stir it well and let stand for 20 minutes for the fruit to settle. Stir and ladle into clean, dry, warm jars. Seal at once with waxed paper discs, wiping the necks of the jars with a clean, damp cloth if necessary. Close with a lid or appropriate cover.

Let cool, label and store in a cool, dark cupboard until required.

VARIATION BLACKCURRANT AND RHUBARB JAM
Rhubarb combines well with soft fruit such as blackcurrants, raspberries and strawberries, giving them more body and reducing the seediness of the fruit. Use half soft fruit and half rhubarb, and omit the ginger.

Berries make a marvellous seedless jam – use sweet ones like strawberries and raspberries, blackberry-raspberry crosses like the Scottish tayberry or the Californian loganberry, then something sharp such as cranberries or red or blackcurrants. In season, every other farm gateway sets out 'pick-your-own' signs. Early summer is the time to enjoy these soft fruits fresh – and to make this jelly, which is delicious spread in the middle of a plain Victoria sponge cake or dissolved in boiling water for a warming winter drink.

RED BERRY JELLY

500 g strawberries

500 g raspberries or redcurrants

500 g loganberries or tayberries

500 g blackcurrants

freshly squeezed juice of 1 lemon

500 ml water

sugar or preserving sugar (see method)

a jelly bag or muslin

2–3 clean, dry, warm jam jars (page 4), 250 ml each, with lids or covers

waxed paper discs

makes 500–750 ml

Put all the fruit (no need to strip currants) in a large preserving pan with the lemon juice and water and bring slowly to the boil. Part-cover with a lid and simmer until the fruit has softened, 10–15 minutes. Transfer to a jelly bag or muslin suspended over a large bowl and leave to drip all night.

Measure the juice into a clean preserving pan and, for every 600 ml of juice, add 450 g sugar. Set over low heat and bring to simmering point, dissolving the sugar, stirring all the while. When it has dissolved, increase the heat and boil hard for 5–10 minutes until setting point is reached.

Take the pan off the heat and test for set (page 129). If the jelly is not ready, put the pan back on the heat to boil for a few minutes, then test again. Repeat this process if necessary and remember to take the pan off the heat during testing because over-boiling will ruin it.

When setting point has been reached, skim the jelly with a perforated skimmer. Stir the jelly and ladle into warm, clean, dry jars. Wipe the necks of the jars with a clean, damp cloth. Seal at once with waxed paper discs, placed directly on top of the jelly. Seal the jars. Let cool, label and store in a cool, dark cupboard until required.

VARIATION You can make this jelly with redcurrants, blackcurrants or any single soft fruit.

The beauty of this marmalade is that it can be made in small quantities at any time of the year, not just when Sevilles are in season. The quantities given here yield two or three jars, but if you want to make it in bulk, then simply double or treble the ingredients. Cut the peel to suit your taste – thick or thin by hand, chunky or fine using a blender.

LEMON, LIME AND GRAPEFRUIT MARMALADE

1 unwaxed lemon

1 small unwaxed pink grapefruit

1 unwaxed lime

500 ml water

freshly squeezed juice of ½ lemon

1 kg sugar

3 clean, dry, warm jam jars (page 4), about 250 g each, with lids or covers

waxed paper discs

makes 500–750 g

Scrub the fruit and prise out any stalk ends still attached. Put in a pan and cover with cold water. Set over low heat and cook until tender, 1½–2 hours. The fruit is ready when it 'collapses'. Lime zest is much tougher than other citrus peel, so you must make sure it is tender at this stage.

Transfer the fruit to a chopping board and, when cool enough to handle. cut in half, scrape out all the flesh and pips and add to the pan of water. Bring to the boil and simmer for 5 minutes. Cut the zest into strips as thin as possible, or put it in a blender and blend until chunky. Strain the water from the pips and flesh and return it to the pan, adding the chopped zest and the lemon juice. Discard the pips and debris.

Add the sugar to the pan and bring slowly to simmering point, stirring until the sugar has dissolved. Because the sugar content is high, this will take quite a long time. When the marmalade has become translucent, you will know the sugar has dissolved and you can increase the heat. Bring to the boil and boil rapidly until setting point is reached, 5–10 minutes.

Take the pan off the heat and test for set (page 129). If the marmalade is not ready, put the pan back on the heat to boil for a few minutes longer and test again. Repeat this process if necessary and remember to take the pan off the heat during testing because over-boiling will ruin it.

When setting point has been reached, return to simmering point, then turn off the heat. Skim with a perforated skimmer, stir well and let stand for 30 minutes for the fruit to settle. Stir and ladle into clean, dry, warm jars and wipe the necks of the jar with a clean, damp cloth if necessary. Seal at once with waxed paper discs and covers.

Let cool, label and store in a cool, dark cupboard until required.

Chutney, a cherished sweet and spicy condiment on the British table, is an Anglo-Indian remnant from the days of the East India Company and the Raj. Homemade versions have always been popular in England – just another aspect of the national taste for jams and pickles to serve with bread, cheese and cold meats. They have acquired a distinctively British flavour, different from their originals in India. Though some sweet chutneys are made there, in fact authentic Indian chutneys are often more akin to relishes. The fresh coconut and lentil varieties of South India, for example, are freshly made for each meal.

PLUM CHUTNEY

800 g plums, about 14, stoned and chopped

225 g raisins

1 large onion, chopped

½ teaspoon sea salt

150 ml cider vinegar

½ teaspoon ground ginger

a good pinch of freshly grated nutmeg

140 g sugar or brown sugar

PICKLING SPICE MIX

1½ teaspoons coriander seeds

1 teaspoon allspice berries

½ teaspoon whole cloves (about 10)

¼ teaspoon black peppercorns

¾ teaspoon mustard seeds (yellow or brown)

2 preserving jars with non-metal lids, 500 ml each, sterilized (page 4)

2 waxed paper discs

makes 800 ml

To make the pickling spice mix, put the coriander seeds, allspice berries, cloves, peppercorns and mustard seeds in a muslin bag and tie it or in a meshed spice ball.

Put the plums, raisins, onion and salt in a stainless steel preserving pan or heavy-based saucepan (never use a copper pan to make chutney as it will react with the vinegar). Stir in the vinegar, then add the ball or bag of pickling spices. Bring to the boil, reduce the heat and simmer gently for about 40 minutes, stirring occasionally. Be careful not to scorch the chutney as it cooks and thickens.

Add the ginger, nutmeg and sugar and mix well. Keep a close eye on the chutney and cook for another 10–15 minutes, stirring regularly to make sure it doesn't burn. It should be dark and tangy yet sweet and thick. As it cools and sets, it will become thicker still.

Remove the ball or bag of pickling spices and pour the chutney into the sterilized jars while still hot. Seal at once with waxed paper discs and non-metal lids. Let cool, label and store in a cool, dark cupboard until required.

The best thing about this old country recipe is that it is very simple to make, like most chutneys. Serve in pork sandwiches, as an accompaniment to all kinds of eggs, cheese and cold meats or with a traditional English breakfast.

APPLE CHUTNEY

1 kg cooking apples, peeled and cored

500 g onions, quartered

125 g raisins

125 g sultanas

500 g demerara sugar

½ teaspoon cayenne pepper

½ teaspoon hot dry mustard

½ teaspoon ground ginger

25 g sea salt

500 ml malt vinegar, plus 500 ml extra to add as the chutney boils down

4–6 clean, dry, warm jars (page 4), 375 g each, with lids or covers, warmed in a low oven while the chutney is boiling

waxed paper discs

makes 1.5–2.25 kg

Chop the apples and onions very finely – this can be done in a food processor, but take care not to reduce them to a pulp. It is important for the chutney to have texture.

Put the apples, onions, raisins, sultanas, sugar, cayenne, mustard, ginger, salt and the 500 ml malt vinegar in a large pan and simmer for 1–1½ hours over low to medium heat. Stir regularly to make sure the sugar does not burn, adding extra vinegar as necessary as the chutney reduces.

Remove the pan from the heat and let the chutney settle. Stir and pack into warm, clean jars, cover with a waxed disc and seal at once. Let cool, label and store in a cool, dark cupboard for at least 1 month before you try it. This kind of chutney improves with age.

This recipe is based on a traditional Indian pickle where the spices and onion are reduced to a paste, then cooked in vinegar. The sugar and fruit are added towards the end and simmered just for a short while. Hard green fruit is used traditionally, so try to find a hard mango rather than a ripe one. If ripe fruits are used, they will disintegrate too much and the idea is that the pickled fruit should retain its texture. Green or unripe papaya, peach, pear, quince can be also be used to make this recipe. The chutney goes well with spiced stir-fries and casseroles, roast meats, curries and Indian take-away. You could also try it with a baked potato or scrambled eggs.

INDIAN GREEN MANGO CHUTNEY

1 onion (100 g) cut into quarters

2–5 fresh green and red chillies (to taste), halved and deseeded

1 egg-sized piece of fresh ginger, peeled and cut into quarters

2 garlic cloves, peeled

30 g mixed mustard seeds

15 g cumin seeds

2 teaspoons ground turmeric

½ teaspoon sea salt

200 ml white wine vinegar

1 tablespoon olive oil

100 g sugar

600 g green mangoes or other under-ripe fruit, cut into 1 cm cubes

4 small, clean, dry, warm jars (page 4), 200 ml each, with lids or covers

waxed paper discs or greaseproof paper

makes 800 ml

Put the onion, chillies, ginger, garlic, mustard and cumin seeds, turmeric and salt in a blender. Add 2–3 tablespoons of the vinegar and grind to a paste.

Put the oil in a saucepan, add the paste and cook over low heat for 10 minutes, adding the remaining vinegar as the paste cooks down. Add the sugar and continue cooking over low heat until it has dissolved.

Add the fruit to the pan, stir well and simmer until just tender but not soft, about 10 minutes. Spoon the chutney into clean, dry, warm jars, cover with waxed paper discs or greaseproof paper, then seal. Let cool, label and store in a cool, dark cupboard until required.

INDEX

CREDITS

PHOTOGRAPHY

Key: a=above, b=below, r=right, l=left, c=centre

Martin Brigdale: 1, 16r, 20, 21c & r, 24, 25r, 48al, 50, 60, 86cr & br, 99–100, 105–110, 115–116, 123

Peter Cassidy: 23al, 25l & c, 27a, 48bl & r, 57–58, 63–65, 66 (excluding br), 69, 74, 78–81, 86bl, 89–91, 113, 120–121, 124, 126al, 136

Jean Cazals: 8ar

Tara Fisher: 6, 126 (excluding al), 128–135, 138–141

Christine Hanscombe: 23br

Jeremy Hopley: 48ar, 54–55

Caroline Hughes: 8al, 12, 15, 144

Tom Leighton: 21l

William Lingwood: endpapers, 2–3, 8bc, 10, 11b, 17a & b inset, 18, 32–37, 72–73, 82, 86al & ar, 92–97

Diana Miller: 102

David Montgomery: 8br, 14

David Munns: 71

Claire Richardson: 11a

Debi Treloar: 26, 27b

Pia Tryde: 4–5, 8bl, 13acr, 16cl, 23ar & bl

Ian Wallace: 28–30, 38–43, 48ac, 52, 66br, 77, 85, 118

Philip Webb: 44–46

Alan Williams: 16cr

Francesca Yorke: 8ac, c & lc, 13 (excluding acr), 16l & c, 17 background, 19

RECIPES

VATCHARIN BHUMICHITR is a well-known chef and author of numerous books on Thai cooking. His London restaurants have always been listed in the Top Ten Thai restaurants in Britain, and he recently opened a restaurant in Miami, Tamarind Thai Restaurant.

Papaya salad with squid

MAXINE CLARK has taught in well-known cooking schools such as Leith's in London, and now teaches at Alastair Little's Tasting Places in Sicily and Tuscany. Her work appears regularly in magazines and newspapers.

Apricot tart
Caramelized pears with marsala and
*   mascarpone cream*
Classic lemon tart
Curd cheese and cherry strudels
Lychee and coconut cheesecakes
Orange, endive and black olive salad
Parma ham with figs
Pineapple and passion fruit curd tartlets
Red mullet and blood oranges cooked in a parcel
Tangerine and chocolate cheesecake

LINDA COLLISTER is the author of three landmark titles on baking and two hugely popular books on chocolate—all were bestsellers around the world. Her easy-to-follow, delicious recipes have made her the doyenne of baking.

Banana pecan loaf
Cranberry, orange and pecan muffins
Citrus summer cake
Easy chocolate and blackberry roulade

MANISHA GAMBHIR HARKINS is Features Editor of *The Master's Table* magazine and was Guild of Food Writers' Food Journalist of the Year in 1999. She has also appeared on TV and radio.

Lamb and apricot tagine
Plum chutney
Sweet potato and banana spice fritters

KATE HABERSHON is Food Editor of *Cosmopolitan* magazine. She is now a food stylist and food editor: her work appears in many leading magazines and commercials and on television.

Overnight pancakes with tropical fruit and mango
*   and ginger purée*
Raspberry waffles with peach and pistachio honey
Spicy nut waffles with ginger pears

JANE NORAIKA is head chef at London's most celebrated vegetarian restaurant, Food for Thought, where she indulges her passion for cooking good food with fine ingredients that just happen to be meat-free. She has produced two cookbooks for the restaurant.

Exotic fruit scrunch
Strawberry and mascarpone trifle
Summer brioche pudding

ELSA PETERSEN-SCHEPELERN is a Danish-Australian food writer. Her delicious recipes are inspired by an eclectic mix of cuisines, as well as fresh seasonal ingredients.

Rockmelon soup with Japanese pink pickled ginger
Thai mango beef salad
Watermelon soup with chilli flakes

LOUISE PICKFORD is a British food writer, now living and working in Sydney, who has worked all around the world. She is a regular contributor to several magazines, including *Food and Travel* and *delicious* and is the author of more than a dozen cookery books.

Blackberry buttermilk pancakes
Duck with spiced plums

Fig, goats' cheese and prosciutto skewers
Fresh figs with ricotta and honeycomb
Honey-roasted peaches with ricotta and coffee
*   bean sugar*
Mango cheeks with spiced palm sugar ice cream
Mini pork and apple pies
Pork steaks with apple and blackberry compote
Tea-smoked Asian spiced duck breast with mango
*   and sesame salsa*
Warm blueberry and almond muffins
Warm compote with peaches, apricots and
*   blueberries*

SONIA STEVENSON is one of the great chefs of Britain and her restaurant, the Horn of Plenty in Devon, won huge accolades. She often appears on TV, and is a judge on BBC's *Masterchef.*

Chicken tagine with quinces and preserved lemons

LINDA TUBBY is a leading London food writer and food stylist. Her work appears in magazines such as *Food and Travel*, *BBC Good Food* and *Food Illustrated*.

Feta salad with watermelon
Fig on a cushion with thyme-scented syrup
Fruity lamb stew with basil and coriander
Grilled chilli herb polenta with papaya mojo
Lemongrass-ginger syrup with dragon's eyes
Summer fruit salad with kaffir lime sorbet

LAURA WASHBURN was born in Los Angeles. She trained at the prestigious Paris cooking school, Ecole de Cuisine La Varenne, and worked with Patricia Wells, author of *A Food Lover's Guide to Paris*. She is now based in London, where she translates French cookbooks into English, and writes her own easy, modern recipes.

Rhubarb clafoutis
Simple apple tart
Tender brined chicken with honey-thyme
*   roasted lemons*

LINDY WILDSMITH is well known from her appearances in the celebrity kitchen at *House & Garden* fairs. She has her own cooking school and works with famous chef Franco Taruschio, formerly of the legendary Walnut Tree restaurant, staging popular hands-on Italian lunch party cooking days.

Apple chutney
Indian green mango chutney
Lemon, lime and grapefruit marmalade
Red berry jelly
Rhubarb and ginger jam
Strawberry jam